WOMEN
WHO
MEAN
BUSINESS

Published by CelebrityPress™, Orlando, FL
A division of The Celebrity Branding Agency®

Celebrity Branding® is a registered trademark
Printed in the United States of America.

ISBN: 9780983947080
LCCN: 2012933673

This publication is designed to provide accurate and authoritative information with regard to the subject matter covered. It is sold with the understanding that the publisher is not engaged in rendering legal, accounting, or other professional advice. If legal advice or other expert assistance is required, the services of a competent professional should be sought. The opinions expressed by the authors in this book are not endorsed by CelebrityPress™ and are the sole responsibility of the author rendering the opinion.

Most CelebrityPress™ titles are available at special quantity discounts for bulk purchases for sales promotions, premiums, fundraising, and educational use. Special versions or book excerpts can also be created to fit specific needs.

For more information, please write:

CelebrityPress™
520 N. Orlando Ave, #2
Winter Park, FL 32789
or call 1.877.261.4930

Visit us online at www.CelebrityPressPublishing.com

WOMEN
WHO
MEAN
BUSINESS

Contents

CHAPTER 1

INTUITION: Your Secret Talent for Business

By Lee Milteer

It's been taught by great teachers in history that all the answers you really need are within yourself. I grew up on a ranch where I was taught to look past logic and instead, listen to and feel my intuition to know how to deal with life. There were times where we would have an animal that would look like it was perfectly well, but you would intuitively know something was wrong with it. When the vet came, it proved to be true that the animal was sick. Growing up on a ranch helped me develop intuition, which has served me very well today in business.

Because I use my intuition and do what I feel I should do *(instead of what my brain or others have told me was right)*, I have lived my life with great success and prosperity. I have painfully learned that if I do not listen to my inner voice, I nearly always regret my actions and there's hell to pay.

How many times have you left home in the morning when it was beautiful outside, the sun was shining, and the forecast was for a clear day, but something inside of you kept saying *"take an umbrella?"* You ignored your inner nudging and before the end of the day, it was pouring! How many times have you hired someone or bought something when you knew it was not going to work out, but you went through with it anyway? Well I know the answer. We have all done things where inside we got the "message" that we should not do it, but there was someone pushing the "reasons" we should. We go against our own nature and end up paying the price for ignoring our own inner knowledge and wisdom.

I had an experience when I didn't listen to my intuition when I needed to find a replacement for my business manager. I was about to leave for a speaking tour and needed someone to run my office while I was gone. I found someone who looked fabulous on paper and had great references, but there was a little nagging feeling inside that said: *keep looking*. Instead of listening, I let logic and urgency make my decision and I hired her. After I left town she disappeared and left my office in total chaos. If I had honored my intuition and not rushed into making a decision, I would not have had to deal with the massive problems she left me. I learned the hard way that when you're hiring people and doing business, if you don't feel good about them, don't hire them. If it feels wrong, don't do business with someone, regardless of their credentials or how well they represent themselves. You might want to remember the ancient teaching: "*Things are Not Always as They Appear.*"

I have learned to listen to my feelings BEFORE I take action. We live in an unpredictable world and we need to make better decisions. I use a formula that you can benefit from. You might want to write this down and put it where you can see it daily:

HEAD—HEART—GUT—CHECK

Pause, check out your Head, Heart, and Gut before acting or ever making any type of important decision. This makes common sense when you think of it. Make it a habit to ask and check your indicators before you go forth on a choice. Your reliable indicators are your head, your intellect, your heart, your feelings, and your gut. They warn you about danger.

Head: I ask questions about situation, problem, or challenge. I use my conscious mind to discern questions I need answered. For example, is this person telling me the truth?

Heart: I listen to my heart and ask: is this the right direction for me? Do I naturally feel attracted to this? Am I hearing truth? The internal part of yourself, the voice inside tells you when things feel right or wrong. For example, my heart is 'my feelings'. Am I relaxed around the person I am asking the question about (Is this person telling me the truth?) or do I feel uptight and uncomfortable? Keep in mind that your body does talk to you. For me personally, if I feel shut down, tight, and not good, I know something is not right. However, if I feel open, lighthearted, and relaxed, I trust that my "heart" is telling me all is well. You have to pay attention to your own signals.

Gut: Trust your "gut feeling". If it doesn't feel right, chances are, it's not right for you. What may be right for one person can be wrong for the next person. Your gut instinct, your inner voice, is always there for you when you take the time to pay attention and listen.

GO WITH YOUR FIRST CHOICE

When you want to ask yourself a question, it would be good for you to always LISTEN TO YOUR FIRST IMPRESSION. This is because your intuition is able to communicate more clearly BEFORE you begin to cloud your mind with all sorts of other details. When you're clouding your mind up like this, you are focusing more on the conscious part of your brain (ruled by the subconscious or unconscious part of your brain). Fear and indecision can then run rampant and deliver incorrect information. This leads to a decision based upon partial, tainted information. Your intuition knew the answer BEFORE this clouding began. Trust your first choice.

DON'T "FORCE" DECISIONS

That's right; there are times when perhaps you should not make an instant decision, and you must give yourself permission to wait. If you are confused about an issue then your decision will be confused, and you don't want to make decision when you aren't clear. Learn to relax, let the situation go, turn it over to your subconscious mind, and let it go to work for you. Your subconscious mind knows a lot more than you may give it credit for, so please learn to trust it. It keeps your body systems running 24 hours a day, seven days a week, and is always paying attention. Let the decision go for right now and the answer will come to you.

BE OPEN TO ANSWERS THAT MAY SURPRISE YOU

The purpose of developing awareness of your intuition is that it helps keep you safe in all ways. Think of your sixth sense as a power that encapsulates a dimension of awareness outside of space and time that gives you extrasensory perception that, when developed and used, allows you to make much better choices both in business and in your personal life.

Now more than ever when you deal with people, you must learn to use your instincts and tune in to feel the true nature of the other person's intent. When you use your intuition correctly, you will be able to read the unsavory energies of morally bankrupt people's lies and deceptions. When you take time to read between the lines, you can avoid a great deal of heartache in the future. Pay attention and listen to these people with your intuition and not just analyze what they say and do. Remember to pause and check out your Head, Heart, and Gut before acting.

Famous people like Isaac Newton and Albert Einstein felt that using their sixth sense helped them find answers and solutions to problems that they could not find in their normal state of mind. Most millionaires and highly successful people from all over the world have shared over and over how they use their intuition or sixth sense to determine what choices they make.

I would like to suggest that we all reach beyond the mundane thinking we have been programmed with, thinking that has often lulled us into docile acquiescence. Sadly, most of our childhood programming has disempowered us to look for inner talents to know things. We must give ourselves permission to live life on grander terms that will lead to a better quality of life by opening our minds. Each one of us has built-in abilities to know things that are not always logical.

We have abilities to know if deals or decisions will work out well for us if we take the time to stop and feel BEFORE we take action or sign that deal. We have to take the time to develop and trust these inner talents.

If you sincerely want to develop these talents, you have to let go of your ego for awhile and be open-minded to trying new ways of thinking and feeling. We have to face the facts of life that the old programming we received from society has not encouraged the use of the sixth sense. Not using our intuition has left us in a mess, often times trusting people who have not deserved our trust and who have had their own personal greedy agendas.

We have been programmed to be so logical and analytical in our thinking that we forget our intuitive abilities. It's seriously dangerous to not pay attention to the inner messages in the troubled world we are operating in today. It's just good risk management to pay attention to our sixth sense!

KICK START YOUR INTUITION

You don't have to be sitting in your office to come up with creative and intuitive solutions! First, outline exactly what solution you need. For example: You have interviewed several new possible candidates for a position. It appears to you that they are all equally qualified according to their resumes. They all passed your internal office tests and you liked them all equally. You're stumped as to which one to hire. Who fits in the office the best? Who will be your best choice?

POSSIBLE SOLUTIONS: Before you make your decision, allow your mind to play with each possible choice. When you envision your office in a month, does any one of the choices pop into your mind? Can you SEE that person in your office? If so, do you FEEL HAPPY? Do you feel frustrated when you SEE THEM? Ask your INTUITION to give you a CLEAR SIGN or IMPRESSION ON WHO TO HIRE. (Always remember that your intuition wants you to ASK for help). Then let it go for a while. Now relax and let it go. Then allow yourself to play, take a walk, or just enjoy nature. Hang out with your pets, kids, or something that engages your creative right brain. Ask it out loud to help you find solutions and then wait for inspiration if you can. Play hooky for an hour and then come back to work on the problem.

> *Now More Than Ever When You Deal With People, You Must Learn To Use Your Instincts And Tune In To Feel The True Nature Of The Other Person's Intent.*

Adopt a childlike view of the situation. Let go of your ego. Stop being an adult for a few minutes! Children often see the obvious where adults make things harder and more complicated than necessary. Look at the problem from as many different angles as possible. Ask other people. Often times, people who know nothing can give you a gem of an idea that will turn into the real solution!

> *When Trying To Get Information From Your Intuition, Pay Attention To Your Dreams And Your Daydreams: They Are Your Personal, Non-Verbal Imagery*

Intuition likes to be asked for help, so do that often. You cannot get anything wrong when trying new ways to jumpstart your intuition. The real secret is to start communicating with yourself and your intuition. When you take the time to write out the answers you need, or even state out loud that you need help, you jumpstart your intuition to start working on the problem you want answers for right away. Now your job is to look, listen, and feel for the answer.

Intuition should add to good judgment, not replace it. As much as I believe in my sixth sense, I would never allow intuition to be the sole guide in my life, any more than I would allow logic to be the sole guide. I think intuition gives you more data to make good decisions but it's a misconception that it should be used alone to make decisions. Your intuitive abilities help you in effective decision-making when you add other factors in the mix. Sometimes a predominantly linear thinking process might be preferable when clear, empirical knowledge or information is available to you. When you have little data to make a decision but need one right away, an intuitive process may be more efficient.

Yesterday's Learned Beliefs Cannot Solve Today's Challenges or Capitalize on Tomorrow's Opportunities. We simply no longer can take other people's word for truth. The old way of simply trusting other people with our lives and money who may be morally bankrupt is not working. The person that you have to trust is you. You've got to be at a point that you trust your own inner wisdom before you trust anybody else. You must discern truth to prosper in today's world. If you would like to improve your intuitive abilities, please visit my web site: www.leemilteer.com and check out my Audio program, *Intuition: The New Common Sense*. I promise you this resource will give you the tools, skills, and awareness you need to use and trust your instincts and natural abilities to discern truth to capitalize on the opportunities that life has to offer.

Blessings and Light to you

Lee Milteer
Performance Coach

About Lee

Lee is a Performance and Productivity Coach, Author, Professional Speaker, and TV Personality. Lee is known as one of the leading experts in the field of Human potential. She is the founder of the Millionaire Smarts® and Untamed Success Coaching programs. Lee also hosts Untamed Success: Positive TV, a Web-Based TV Show. Lee speaks all over North America and Europe in Conventions, Private Companies, and Entrepreneurial and Niche Market Events. As president of Lee Milteer, Inc., she has counseled and trained over a million people in her speeches. Her clients include: Walt Disney, AT&T, XEROX, IBM, Ford Motor Co., NASA, Federal Express, 3M, Sales & Marketing Executive International, GKIC, and hundreds of government agencies, conventions, and association meetings.

Lee is not only a successful businesswoman, she is also a talented artist, writer, photographer, and painter who has shown and sold her work in galleries and art shows. Lee lives in Virginia Beach, Virginia on the beach with her dog "Angel", Cat "Midnight", and her husband Clifton Williams. Her hobbies are painting, photography and traveling and her favorite charities include the SPCA and animal rescue organizations. She owns her own office building where her Publishing Company Lee Milteer Publishing is located.

In her career, Lee Milteer has shared the platform with many famous personalities, including Dr. Phil, Gene Simmons from KISS, Dan Kennedy, Jack Canfield, Mark Victor Hansen from the Chicken Soup book fame, Tony Robbins, Zig Ziglar, Stephen Covey, Brian Tracy, Ted Koppel, Lynn Redgrave, Marlo Thomas, Robert Cialdini, T. Harv Eker, Mike Ditka, Les Brown, Wally "Famous" Amos, Ivanka Trump, George Foreman, and Joan Rivers, to mention a few.

Lee is a recognized, best-selling audio and video author. She has authored books including: *Success Is An Inside Job* and *Spiritual Power Tools for Successful Selling*, is Co-Author of *Walking with the Wise for Entrepreneurs, Reach Your Career Dreams, The Secrets of Peak Performers One and Two, The Phenomenon: Achieve More in the Next 12 Months than the Previous 12 Years, Ultimate Entrepreneur Success Secrets*, and *Walking with The Wise*

Overcoming Obstacles. Plus she has featured chapters in *Conversations with Female Entrepreneurs* and *The Ultimate Business Advantage.* Lee also writes columns for the GKIC NO B.S Newsletter and Australia's HavaMag Business Magazine.

Lee has been interviewed in newspapers, magazines and trade journals all over the world, including U.S.A. TODAY, Wall Street Journal, Glamour, and Cosmopolitan.

Lee has been an expert guest on more than 700 TV and Radio shows on National and International TV and Radio around the world. Her programs are translated into Japanese, Russian, Dutch and other languages.

Lee hosted and produced her own cable television show, "LifeStyles" and had her own advice segment on Canada's #1 rated daytime talk show, "The Dini Petty Show." In recognition of her achievements, Lee received a Doctorate in Motivational Theory from Commonwealth College and she has won many awards for her Entrepreneurial Business Success.

Please go to: www.leemilteer.com and sign up for Lee Milteer's Untamed Success Weekly newsletter.

CHAPTER 2

My Non-Negotiable Truths for Women Who Aspire To Be Entrepreneurs

By Kimberly Martinez

I'll never forget thinking it was odd that my boss had scheduled a meeting in MY office. We always met in his. When he walked in the door at our scheduled meeting time, the combination of the uncomfortable look on his face, along with the "pink slip" in his hand, told me I was about to lose my job.

The reaction I had to the news was unexpected. I think the reason he met in my office was that he expected me to be upset and wanted me to have my privacy. After all, I was the primary breadwinner in a family with three kids under the age of three and the job market was in the pits in the post 9-11 environment. Instead, as I saw his mouth moving and he told me I was being laid off, I only heard the words of Martin Luther King Jr. echoing in my head saying "Free At Last, Free at Last, Oh Dear Lord, I'm free at last."

The truth is, I had always aspired to be an entrepreneur, but had never been brave enough to make the leap from the corporate safety net. But I didn't make the decision to leave my job – my former employer did it for me. What for many people would

23

have been a terrifying moment became one of the most liberating days of my life.

Fast forward nearly 10 years later and I am living the life I had always dreamed of. Today I am the proud CEO and Co-Founder of Bonitas International. Our firm is a fashion accessories company that creates specialty jewelry for women who have to wear employee ID badges or conference credentials. Last summer, we sold our 1 millionth "BooJeeBead"™, the beaded ID necklace concept my partner Lisa Harrington cleverly created that was the first product we introduced. Today we have over 500 products which are sold at over 4000 retail stores in North America as well as in big box retail stores and on our websites: www. BooJeeBeads.com and www.EyeGlassHolders.com. We have gotten tremendous media attention with our innovative product collection, and we have been featured in every major newspaper and television network in the US, including stints on the Today Show and HSN!

So often people approach me and share with me **their** desire to start their own business and ask for my advice. I share with them my *non-negotiable truths for women who aspire to be entrepreneurs* that I would like to share with you as well.

TRUTH #1. CREATE YOUR MANIFESTO

Seventy percent of all people aspire to be an entrepreneur, and that is a fact. The question for you is — Why? Your manifesto is your personal mission, your values and what drives you forward, all wrapped up into a one-page summary. To create this guiding light, you need to take the time to do your front work and really spend some time reflecting on your ideal life and what is important to you, and then bring it all together into a clear statement of your principles and priorities.

Look at your current free time and life style. Rank these areas of your life on a scale of one through 100, with 100 being the ideal life you would like to live.

Create an honest assessment of your life, including your personal and financial responsibilities, and create a one-page sheet that lists your assets from your home and car to your savings and retirement account funds – to be able to identify cash available to fuel your start up. Put a realistic monthly budget on paper so you truly understand what you need to be able to support your current household bills.

Spend some time dreaming about the things that make you really happy.

Create a list of the things that make you unhappy and that you would like to eliminate from your life.

Then pull all these together into a simple one-page document that articulates what your ideal life would look like. For examples please check out: www.KimberlyMartinez.com/manifesto

TRUTH #2. IT'S ALL ABOUT THE MONEY, HONEY...

Access to capital is the biggest issue most small business owners deal with, but there are still strategies you can use to get access to the critical funds you can use to start and grow your business. The fact is, it isn't easy to borrow money anymore – banks don't fund good ideas... only businesses that are making money. Most of us have had our credit card limits slashed, and the strategy of running up and/or maxing out the limits on your personal credit cards is dangerous, given the credit score obsession of the banks and other lenders. Here are some steps you MUST implement:

It is critical that you aggressively manage and monitor your credit scores because any lending sources will dramatically diminish if your credit score is not attractive. There are many websites available that provide this service. Just make sure you use one that monitors all three Credit Bureaus.

A little known trick is that you can borrow up to 50% of your active 401Ks (not your IRAs but your 401Ks), typically up to 50k at very attractive interest rates AND that loan does not show up on your credit report, so it helps you to keep your credit score healthy and can provide startup capital to get your business up and running while allowing you to pay back the loan over an extended period of time. Contact your 401K provider at your workplace to learn more about the availability of the loan program, and your tax and financial advisor to evaluate whether this choice is right for you.

There are a number of alternative lending marketplaces – often called peer-to-peer lending or crowdsourcing available, that will loan funds typically up to $25,000. Interests rates vary based on your credit score but check out sites like: www.Prosper.com and www.LendingClub.com.

TRUTH #3. PLAN SIMPLY

One of the next tips is that people get caught up in putting together huge business plans. I am a big fan of the book — *The One Page Business Plan* by Jim Horan, which is now available with an interactive CD to help make planning even easier (http://www. onepagebusinessplan.com/). The basic steps of getting started seem so overwhelming and business plans evolve so often that doing a big plan is a waste of time and energy. The truth is your business plan will change as you and your business do, but you DO need to be able to answer the basic questions addressed in the one page business plan to enable your business to succeed.

TRUTH #4. JOIN A TRIBE

Being an entrepreneur can be a lonely place. To help ease some of that sense of isolation, it is critical you join a group that allows you to connect with other like-minded individuals. I am not talking about a networking group where people go to lunch and exchange business cards for the purposes of generating business, but rather a group of similar professionals who can provide support in the areas you lack experience. Exposure to that group, before you fully launch, will give you a lot of insight and the knowledge you need to be successful. Your currency in these groups is your ability to provide support for other members in your areas of expertise. In my case, for example, I was an expert in marketing and distribution but was clueless about the basics I needed to understand to run a business. I was able to get many of my questions answered, and received solid advice from professionals by joining the Make Mine A Million organization, which has been a tremendous resource. I am able to offer advice to others in my area of expertise in exchange for information in areas where I may be in over my head. You can learn more about this organization for women business owners at www.Make-MineAMillion.org.

Other organizations include Entrepreneurs Organization at: www.EONetwork.org or the National Federation Independent Business owners at: www.NFIB.org

TRUTH #5. MANAGE YOUR FEAR

You have to learn to manage your emotions - specifically your fear - as you embark upon your new journey. Emotions will play a huge part in your ability — or inability — to be successful. I call it "managing the chattering monkeys in your mind." It is like Henry Ford's famous quote "Whether you think you can, or you can't, you are right."

Many successful business owners I know have engaged the services of a life or business coach at some point in the process. One resource I really like is available at the Coach Connection: www.TheCoachConnection.com. They have a program that enables you to experience one-on-one coaching — trial sessions with three coaches before you choose the one that is right for you. Whatever approach you choose, you have to find some resource/process to help you keep your mind positive and to deal with the inevitable fear that comes from sailing off into unchartered territory.

TRUTH #6. YOU NEED TO GET YOUR LOVED ONES ENROLLED IN YOUR DREAM

Your choice to start your own business is scary and risky. You're going out on your own and it requires you to rethink your partnerships and the responsibilities that go with them in your personal life - and that needs a lot of groundwork. Many people get their spouses/partners involved in their business. I am not a fan of this for two reasons. First, you need to have at least one person in your household that has a predictable income to minimize financial stress, Secondly, the pressures of being co-workers is very difficult on a marriage. Whether or not you choose to work together in the new business, you MUST take the time to talk to your family to get them engaged and behind your vision. This will help them be both comfortable and as supportive as possible. You will need a team behind you that believes in you as you venture out onto your brave new journey.

TRUTH #7. DECIDE IF YOU ARE GOING TO WORK ON YOUR BUSINESS, OR IN YOUR BUSINESS?

One of the challenges most businesses owners face is the endless number of tasks that need to be done. Many businesses get stuck because the owner spends all their time and energy doing task-focused work instead of setting the vision and leading the business to success. This is due to the fact that most businesses start at the kitchen table and usually have little to no staff to begin with (other than supportive family and friends). Accepting help from others and hiring staff at the first opportunity is a non-negotiable for success.

If you want to make the leap from dreamer to doer, set your sight on your intention, be smart enough to ask for help every step of the way, and be brave enough to follow your dreams.

My partner Lisa Harrington and I did all of those steps and today live the life of our dreams. We wish the same for you and your family. Best of luck and enjoy the journey!

About Kimberly

Kimberly Martinez is a former Fortune 50 top executive who built and drove marketing and distribution systems for some of the most respected companies in the U.S. After losing her job in the travel industry following the events of September 11, 2001, Kimberly joined forces with her sister-in-law, Lisa Harrington, in 2002 to create Bonitas International, the home of BooJeeBeads™. The firm's flagship product line is a collection of fashion ID jewelry that lets women wear their employee ID or conference credentials with style. The products can be found in 4,000 retail outlets across North America as well as on the company's websites: www.BooJeeBeads.com and www.EyeGlassHolders.com

Kimberly has been seen everywhere – from The Today Show's couch to meeting with Vogue fashion editor André Leon Talley at New York's Fashion Week. Her business advice has been featured in USA Today, The New York Times, The Wall Street Journal, Forbes and Entrepreneur, as well as Smart Money, Reader's Digest and BusinessWeek. She has appeared on the Today Show, NBC, CBS, ABC, Fox, MSNBC and HSN, and is a Make Mine a Million $ Business Awardee as well as a finalist for the 2009 Fortune "10 Most Powerful Women in Small Business" award.

Kimberly resides in Sarasota, FL. She is a graduate of the University of Cincinnati and the UCLA Anderson School of Management. Her first book, The Next Big Thing, soared to the best seller list the day it was released! She is passionate about helping entrepreneurs live the life of their dreams. You can learn more about her at: www.KimberlyMartinez.com

CHAPTER 3

Copywriting Secrets: 3 Secrets for Turning Leads into Clients

By Michele Pariza Wacek
(aka Michele PW)

Let me tell you about Jane.

Jane wanted to start her own online business. It made sense – she was a busy mom and wanted a flexible schedule to work around her family, plus she dreamed of building a business around helping people and making the world a better place. People have been telling her for years she should be getting paid for what she willingly did for free. So why not turn her passion into profit?

And having an online business made sense too. Everyone said marketing online was the cheapest, easiest way to go. Plus she could set her own hours and work when and where she wanted. It was a win-win.

Clearly she needed to get a website up (an online business does require a website after all). So she took a couple of weeks and did just that. Then she sat back and waited.

…And waited.

…And waited.

A few months passed and nothing happened. No leads, no sales. Not even a phone call or an email.

Hmm…Maybe she was wrong to save a few bucks. Maybe she needed a professional. She really didn't like her website anyway, it wasn't all that attractive. So she contacted a company and they put together a gorgeous-looking website. She even sprung for a really beautiful logo to go along with the site. It cost a pretty penny, but that's okay. You gotta' spend money to make money, right?

Well…

The problem was, that gorgeous, expensive website wasn't doing any better than her little, cheap, homemade website. Still no leads, sales or customers. But now she felt even worse, because she was out a big wad of cash and had nothing to show for it.

I've heard stories like Jane's all the time. Entrepreneurs drop thousands of dollars on a pretty but ineffective website. The site has attractive colors, an expensive logo, and probably some sort of flash introduction. (Flash is what looks like animation on websites.) All the money went into graphic designers and/ or web designers. If they spent any money on the writing, it was probably the cheapest part of the bill.

Unfortunately, pretty doesn't sell. (Neither does Flash. Nor expensive logos.)

So what DOES sell? Direct response copywriting.

Let's start with the definition. Copywriting is writing promotional copy – NOT copyrighting something to protect intellectual property (note the difference in spelling copywrite/copyright). If you're in the business of copyrighting intellectual property, you either work for the government or you're an attorney. If you're in the business of copywriting, then you're in the business of writing promotional materials that sell products or services.

If you're like many entrepreneurs, when it comes to writing the copy on your website, your first response is: "That's not such a big deal. I can write. Why should I pay someone to do that?"

Well, that's true. I'm sure you can write. But, (and this is a big but), can you write words that will persuade people to take action? … Ones that will cause people to whip out their wallets in a frenzy because they can't wait to throw money at you?

Oh, you can't?

Well, that's why you need to understand direct response copywriting.

Take junk mail. That's an excellent example of direct response copywriting. Junk mail (also known as direct mail) is designed to get a response from the recipients all by its little self. It's like a sales person, except you don't pay it a salary, benefits or even need to give it vacation. It works 24/7/365 with nary a complaint. And, as it works, it continually brings in leads, customers and sales.

The beauty is the direct mail letter does all the heavy lifting for you. (That's why it's called direct response, because prospects directly respond to the promotional materials.)

But direct response copywriting is not limited to direct mail. You can (and should) use it on your website. Because when you do, you'll find you end up getting more leads, sales and customers from your site.

And isn't that the point of a website? To have it be a sales tool?

Better yet, once you master the basics of direct response copywriting, there's no end to where you can use it. Send an email to your prospect list. Place an ad in a trade magazine. Drop your customers a postcard or letter. You can use direct response to both gain customers and deepen your relationship with them – so they not only buy once from you, but they buy multiple things

AND they tell all their friends about you.

Now, you might be thinking to yourself "…but I HATE junk mail and those really sales-y websites that are all hype-y and inauthentic. Is that what I have to do to sell?"

Well, yes and no.

Look, here's the dirty little secret of direct response copywriting. IF you do it right, it won't sound the least bit sales-y or hype-y to your prospects (but it might sound sales-y or hype-y to people who aren't your prospects). And, of course, if you do it wrong or badly it will certainly sound inauthentic and hype-y to everyone.

So how do you craft direct response copy the right way? Here are three tips to get you started:

TIP #1. Know who you're talking to. You need to both identify and understand your prospects. I like to call these people your ideal clients or your favorite clients rather then target market or niche market.

Why ideal clients? Ideal clients are about connecting with your prospects on a deep, personal level. It's about discovering what makes them tick and talking to them at that deep level (like you would a good friend).

Target market or niche market is more about the external. You define it using things like demographics – 30 to 50 year-old women who are single and are actively dating and looking for a relationship.

Target markets or niche markets are a good place to start – it's a lot easier to get demographic or external data then their attitude and core beliefs. But it doesn't go far enough. Plus, if you only focus on target markets, you run the risk of sounding hype-y and sales-y.

You see, the key to writing strong, compelling, persuasive copy that doesn't sound inauthentic to your prospects is to connect with them on a deep, personal level. And the only way to connect with them at that level is to write to your ideal client rather than your target market.

So what is an ideal client? Let's take that 30-50 year-old woman who is single and actively dating and looking for a relationship.

In that target market there are a number of ideal clients, including (but not limited to):

1. Women who are looking for a fun, easy-going relationship – nothing serious or long term.
2. Women looking for their soulmate.
3. Women looking to get married and don't care if it's their soulmate or not, they just want to be married.
4. Women looking to get married and have given up finding their soulmate for whatever reason, but they still secretly long to be proven wrong and find their soulmate.
5. Women who want to get married and have been damaged/burned so many times they have all sorts of issues they need to work through first.

You get the picture.

So, to put this in business perspective, your copy is going to sound very different if you're targeting women who just want to get married and don't care about finding a soulmate, versus women who want to get married and given up finding their soulmate (but still secretly want one) versus women who need to heal themselves first in order to find a mate (regardless if it's a soulmate or not).

Now, if you don't know which of those groups is your ideal client, then how on earth are you going to be able to write copy that's going to connect to them at their core? You're not. So you're going to write generic-sounding copy that tries to appeal to all those groups (except for maybe the first one) and ends up not appealing to any of them.

Why won't it appeal to any of them? Because they won't feel like it pertains to their specific situation.

Think about it, if you write copy that's so generic it could fit everyone, no one is going to think it will work "for them." Because their situation "is different."

But if you write very specific copy to one group, that all changes. That group will feel like you're talking to directly to them, which means the copy won't feel sales-y or inauthentic to them.

Will it appeal to the other groups? Possibly. But probably not. And that's a good thing too.

How is that a good thing? Because you really only want to attract the people you can help the most. If you're really good at helping women who have given up finding their soulmate actually find their soulmate, and you end up with all these women as customers who either don't care about finding their soulmate or need to heal themselves before even thinking about finding their soulmate, what happens? Not only will you be frustrated working with them, they'll be frustrated working with YOU – not to mention they probably won't get the results they want, which could result in unhappy customers at best and refunds and damage to your reputation at worst.

That's why it's so important to not only figure out who your ideal client is but also make sure you write copy that connects to their core.

TIP #2. Make sure you write benefits, not features. This one is probably the hardest one to "get" but also one of the most critical. People buy benefits, not features, so if you only talk about features you're just asking for people not to buy what you're selling.

So what is the difference between features and benefits? Features are a description of a product – for instance the feature of a weight-loss pill is that it's a pill. No one says "Wa-hoo! I want to take more pills so I'm going to take a weight-loss pill." No. People take weight-loss pills because they want to lose weight and they want it to be easy. The benefit is you want to lose the weight and you want it to be easy. That's why people take weight-loss pills, NOT because it's a pill.

As much as you possibly can, write about WHY someone should buy your product. Think of the solution your product or service provides and write about that.

So how do you write features and benefits? Try this exercise:

Take a piece of paper. Draw a line down the middle. On the left side, list all of the features of your product or service. Go on. List them all. When you think you've thought of them all, come up with three more.

Now on the right side, turn all of those features into benefits. How does this work? Here's an example.

Cell phones are small and portable so you can easily take them everywhere you want to go.

The little word "so" (or "so that" if that's easier for you) will naturally get you thinking about benefits.

And keep going deeper. Just keep asking "so." Like this:

Cell phones are small and portable so you can easily take them everywhere you want to go so you never worry about missing an important call ever again.

Ah. Now we're getting into the real benefit. Why would people want to carry cell phones everywhere? Not because they like the idea of carrying one more piece of technology around with them, but because they want to be able to make a phone call or get a phone call wherever they are. And why do they want to do that? Not because they want to always take phone calls, but because they might miss something if they don't have access to a phone.

That's what you need to do. Get as deep as possible into the benefits. Then, once you know what those benefits are, that's what you tell your customers.

TIP #3. Overcome those objections. This is a biggie. Because the moment you start asking someone for money, objections to giving you money are going to rear its ugly head.

Think of it as a defensive mechanism. There just isn't enough money in the world to buy every little thing. We need to make choices with our money. There's only so much we can buy. And yes, we can always go out and make more, but again we have to make that choice if what we want to buy is worth going out and focusing on making more money.

As you can see, it's not personal. It's a defensive mechanism that allows us to function in our society. So now that you know this, what do you do about it? You have to overcome those objections in your copy.

The biggest objection you need to overcome, no matter what it is you sell, is money. No matter what it costs, there's still going to be an objection. It might be a small objection or a big objection, but it's an objection nevertheless.

What do you do? First, you need to acknowledge it's an objection. Second, you need to show how they're getting so much value for their money it makes no sense for them NOT to purchase it. Third, compare it to something else so your price looks cheap in comparison. For instance, if you're selling a home study course based on your services, you can tell people how much it would cost them to hire you to do XYZ, so in comparison, your product looks cheap.

t that's not the only thing you can compare it to. You can also compare your price to X number of Starbucks vanilla lattes and blueberry scones. This works very well because we're now comfortable with spending $6-$8 on a cup of coffee and scone. It doesn't matter if the comparison doesn't make any sense. It only matters if the price is something we're already comfortable spending, then we can transfer that comfort to what you're selling.

Now if you've enjoyed what you've read here and would like to learn more about copywriting, I have a free gift for you. It's my Copywriting Rescue Kit and it includes a 13-page downloadable white paper plus 2 mp3 audios *5 Psychological Triggers to Turn Prospects Into Clients* and *5 Secrets To Getting All The Business You Can Handle No Matter What the Economy is Doing.* Here's the link: http://www.michelepw.com/freegift

About Michele PW

Considered one of the hottest direct response copywriters and marketing consultants in the industry today, Michele PW (Michele Pariza Wacek), Your $Ka-Ching!$ Marketing Strategist, has a reputation for crafting copy and creating online and offline marketing campaigns that get results.

Michele started writing professionally in 1992, working at agencies and on staff as a marketing/communication/writing specialist. In 1998 she started her business as a freelance copywriter.

But she quickly realized her vision was bigger than serving her clients as a one-woman-shop. In 2004, she began the transformation to building a copywriting company.

Two years later, her vision became a reality. Michele PW/Creative Concepts and Copywriting LLC is the premiere direct response copywriting and marketing company today, catering to entrepreneurs and small business owners internationally, including the "Who's Who" of Internet Marketing.

In addition, Michele is also a national speaker and author, has completed two novels, and is a contributing author to the *Entrepreneur Press Start Up Guide to Information Marketing* and *Trust Your Heart: Transform Your Ideas to Income* (which is also an Amazon Bestseller).

To learn more about Michele and her copywriting and marketing services, you can visit http://www.michelepw.com or call 877-754-3384 x2.

And don't forget to get your free gift, the Copywriting Rescue Kit, which includes a 13-page downloadable white paper plus 2 mp3 audios "5 Psychological Triggers to Turn Prospects Into Clients" and "5 Secrets To Getting All The Business You Can Handle No Matter What the Economy is Doing."

Here's the link: http://www.michelepw.com/freegift

CHAPTER 4

Your Most Important Business Asset: YOU!

By JoLynn Braley

What exactly does it mean to be "a woman who means business"? Can a woman "mean business" without owning a business or without being a business coach?

What about "meaning business" when it comes to taking daily care of your most important asset in your business? That asset being...YOU!

These questions came up for me when sitting down to write this chapter because I'm not a business coach. I do own my own business but it's not a business of teaching others how to become a million-dollar per year business owner.

This statement may shock you, but what I do is *even more important* than teaching you how to run a million-dollar-per-year business and it's what **I** Mean Business About: I am in the business of mentoring spiritual, smart, highly successful (in their business) women to finally achieve success in the one area of their life that has always eluded them: the area of food and their weight.

It's about becoming the YOU you've always known you could be. The YOU who lives IN the body of your dreams, while living the life of your dreams, and doing it with struggle-free action.

41

(Note that the key to permanent, struggle-free success with your body all starts with your Mind - the Mind leads the body. Always.)

Yes, it's a bold statement that the work I do is *even more important* than teaching you how to create a million-dollar business, and here's exactly why my statement is true: **If you don't have a YOU then how can you have that million-dollar business?**

To get specific about it, exactly what is your YOU transported in? That's right – YOU are transported IN your body! And without a YOU, you have no business!

This is something you probably didn't expect to be addressed when it comes to creating an even more successful business than you have now. The truth is that most don't want to talk about it! How you feel about YOU and your own body is not looked at as being the source of why you aren't moving to the next level in your business.

Sure, you could say, "But I have a 'Me' because I do have a body!" and you're right, of course you do. The question though is … what is the *quality* of YOU when you're not feeling good in your own skin? When you're not loving your body? When you're still struggling with food, your weight, and especially with all of those fears you keep trying to stuff down with the food? Those fears of finally going for it in your business, and your life.

Just how heavy does the impact of how you feel about food, your weight, and your body have on ALL areas of your life, including your business? What is the impact to your business when, for example, you feel too fat for the camera, you're not using video to market yourself, and you're not feeling excited about Being Seen?

You know what I mean: You feel fabulous when you schedule in "YOU Time" daily to care for your body and your mind (since the mind leads the body, you must attend to your mind first).

You feel fabulous when you are consistently feeding your body whole, healthy foods, and exercising regularly. You feel especially wonderful to be able to do all of this without struggle! But if you've never experienced living healthy and fit without struggle, don't worry, because most have not. None of my clients did prior to working with me.

When you DO feel fabulous about yourself though, when you feel good in your own skin, feel excited to Be Seen, and are caring for yourself with love and consistency, then it's so much easier for you to do what you need to do in your business, isn't it.

Yes, it's a very simple fact: When you look good you feel good, when you feel good you look good, and when you feel good it's easy for you to take action to grow your business, to Be Seen, because you have the confidence and the belief in yourself to do so!

It's so very simple because you just can't get away from YOU, and you certainly cannot get away from your body. You take it with you everywhere you go and whatever the overall vibe is that you hold about yourself, that vibe colors all other areas of your life. You can't help it because your body and YOU (and how you feel) go with you everywhere.

Here's something even more specific to look at: How does your level of *commitment* to YOU (which shows up in your actions, not your words) and how you care for YOU and your own body directly impact your level of commitment and follow-through in your business? When you're committed to YOU first then it's so much easier to be committed to your business.

However when you're consistently eating junk food, avoiding exercise, not taking the time each day to care for YOU and your body in a healthy, fit way, then your business suffers. You lack the confidence and belief in yourself to get out there and market YOU. You just don't "feel like it", because you truly don't FEEL like it!

Now, in case you might be thinking that maybe you can "get

away with it," meaning that you can keep putting off taking care of YOU and the body you live in, thinking that all you need to do is keep taking action in your business, to push through and then "someday" when you get around to it, you'll attend to your body and YOU.... well, here's why it's so important that you take care of YOU now: it's that old saying you've heard before, "People don't buy your products or services, they buy YOU." Well guess what? It's true!

YOU are your product, your brand, your service. YOU Are Your Business, no matter what kind of business you have and no matter whether you even have a business! Before going any further though, in order to get to that next level in your business you must make it your number one business to step up and become CEO of you and your own body.

How can you expect to become CEO of your own million-dollar business when you're still struggling with food and your weight? *Does that struggle make you feel empowered* and ready to rock the world with your business? Since it does not, then you are not an inner match to the self-empowered CEO you'd love to be!

This addresses the core of YOU, doesn't it. Because as you already know, if you don't believe in, respect, and adore YOU, then how can others believe in, respect, and adore your business (which IS You) and believe in what you have to offer? How can you possibly give what you don't already own?

Now you're probably wondering what's next - how in the world do you get to the place where caring for YOU each day is effortless? How do you consistently live healthy and fit without struggle? How do you get to the place where you feel so good in your own skin that your belief in YOU and your business skyrockets?

Well I'm certain you agree that if you could already do this then you would be doing it now. You'd have no problem whatsoever living IN the body of your dreams without struggle. You'd make time for YOU every single day so that you could finally live as the YOU you've always known you could be.

There are several steps that go into getting this fabulous outcome of finally being done with your lifelong food and weight struggles because in order to achieve permanent weight loss and maintenance without deprivation, dieting, or struggle, you must heal The Root of the symptom (the symptom is your overweight).

You must transform your Inner YOU to match the body and the life you desire on the outside. Do THAT …and then your physical actions on the outside will become effortless. Struggle-free. Guaranteed.

How can this be guaranteed? Because it's Universal Law. Perhaps you've heard of one of the Universal Laws we all live under, the law of attraction. In this Universe of attraction the inner and the outer always match. Always. So if you want to live healthy and fit without struggle, then you must become the YOU on the inside now that matches what you want on the outside!

This is the work that I do with my clients when I mentor them in my step-by-step proven System to permanent weight loss and maintenance. However, here's something extremely important to note immediately: The "how to" doesn't matter unless you first make the decision for yourself that you must **now** achieve lasting success with food and your weight!

You've no doubt noticed the plethora of "how to" information that is on the market today? Of course there is an overabundance of "how to lose weight" information, but beyond that, you're also bombarded with "how to" for any area of your life.

Well, if you have not first made the decision that you shall once and for all get to The Root of your food and weight struggles so that you can achieve permanent release from the struggle, then the "how to" does not matter. Decide first that you shall have the outcome and the "how" will appear. But you won't make that decision until you experience the clarity of exactly what it's costing you to stay where you are.

Therefore I have a very powerful exercise for you to do right now. I invite you to grab your pen and notebook or at least four separate pieces of paper and do this exercise now so that you can gain clarity and take a step forward.

The Big and Bold "Get Real" question for you is: "What exactly is it costing you in all areas of your life to continue living in struggle with food and your weight?"

First, identify how old were you when you first had any kind of struggle with food, body image, weight. Note that you may not have been overweight back then. Next, subtract that age from your current age - that gives you the total number of years you've been struggling with food and your weight.

Then, at the top of each of paper, write:

1. **Business:** What has my [insert # of years] year struggle with food and my weight cost me in my business? (...which includes your finances.)

And, what is it costing me *now* to *keep living* with this struggle?

2. **Relationships:** What has my [insert # of years] year struggle with food and my weight cost me in my relationships? (...which includes family, friends, and your business network.

And, what is it costing me *now* to *keep living* with this struggle?

3. **Spirituality:** What has my [insert # of years] year struggle with food and my weight cost me in my connection to Source Energy/God/The Universe/My Higher Power? (...which includes your spiritual connection and practice, your trust and belief and how you feel about YOU in this Universe.)

And, what is it costing me *now* to *keep living* with this struggle?

4. Body: What has my [insert # of years] year struggle with food and and my weight cost me in my level of health, fitness, and physical well-being? (...which includes everything pertaining to your fitness, food, sports, physical intimacy and health.)

And, what is it costing me *now* to *keep living* with this struggle?

Starting with paper number one, write a detailed list of all of the specific costs to your business that living in the struggle with food and your weight have and are costing you.

You may find that your food and weight struggles are costing you money because you don't market yourself when you feel guilty about how you are eating. Perhaps you feel so bad about your inconsistency to live healthy and fit that you pull back on your email marketing or article marketing, due to severe self-criticism.

Note: if you're doing it in one area of your life, you're doing it in all areas of your life; ...which directly impacts your reach in your marketplace and impacts your income since you're not being heard and Being Seen.

Or you might find that your food and weight struggles are costing you clients, because you lack the confidence to speak your full truth since your belief in yourself erodes every time you "give in" to your cravings for more food when you're not physically hungry. You're unable to believe fully in your own message when your belief in YOU takes a hit every time you break your word to yourself, about how you intend to eat and exercise.

Write down all of the specifics that your unresolved struggles with food and your weight are costing you in your business. When you have filled that paper completely (get another paper if needed!) then go on to the next paper and list all of the ways this ongoing problem has and is costing you in the area of relationships.

Maybe you'll find that you're losing out on opportunities for deeper connection, or for any connection at all if you're single!

Perhaps you hide out at home instead of getting out to socialize with friends and family. If you're single maybe you'll find that your food and weight struggles are costing you enormously because you're hiding behind your computer on dating sites, posting old pictures of yourself and avoiding meeting men face-to-face because then you'd have to face YOU!

Perhaps you're married and have children and you'd love to be a positive role model for them, but instead you turn to food whenever you feel stress over your business. What are all of the specific activities you'd be doing with your family if you were living IN the body of your dreams right now? …and what is it costing you to stay in the struggle instead of living your dream?

What about networking to build business relationships? How are those relationships specifically affected by your lifelong food and weight struggles that continue to affect your self-confidence? And what about your level of intimacy in your committed relationship? That's a large part of a healthy relationship and if you don't even feel attracted to YOU and your body, well what is that costing you?

The area of your spirituality needs to be addressed next, since you're going for a conscious life of balance.

Maybe you've always wanted to fully trust and believe that all is well, that you are a part of this Universe of creation and that everything is always working out for you but instead of doing that, whenever your fears and insecurities come up you turn to food. Which keeps taking you further and further from having any experience of real trust in this Universe (that experience truly comes when things aren't going so well and you're *still able* to trust).

And finally, the last one might be easiest: What exactly is this problem costing you in the area of your health and fitness? What are all of the ways this struggle has been *and now is* impacting your health, your vitality, your strength and agility, your ability to be active, to engage in your favorite sports?

Now go back and read everything you have written. What is the answer you get now to the question, "What exactly has it cost me all these [insert # of years] years, and what exactly is it costing me *now* to *keep living* with this struggle?"

The purpose of doing this exercise was to help you take a big step out of your own way so that you can now have the clarity of where you are. You must know where you are starting in order to decide to take the trip to where you want to be!

And now what? Now you take the next logical action step towards your outcome. (This is another step of the process: clearly defining exactly what you want for your outcome.) After that, I strongly suggest that you build a strong inner foundation of your Inner YOU that will support you in your body, your life, and your business. To do this in the quickest way possible you'll want to follow a step-by-step proven System that others have already followed!

Either way, no matter what costs to your life you uncovered in this Get Real exercise, I trust you can clearly see and feel how important it is that you allow yourself now to become the YOU you've always known you could be – because without that YOU, how can you have the business you've always dreamed of?

You deserve to feel good about YOU, about your life, about your business, and about your body. You deserve to be, do, and have all that you desire, all while feeling good living IN the body of your dreams. Without deprivation, forcing yourself to diet, or struggle.

YOU are your most important business asset and there is nothing you could invest in and "mean business" about that would be more important than YOU.

Here's to Your Best Life...*IN Your Ideal Body!*

About JoLynn

Stop Hiding Behind The Fat™ – Become the YOU You've Always Known You Could Be!

JoLynn Braley, CMNP, The F.A.T. Release Coach, mentors spiritual, high-achieving, six-figure female business owners who want a body that matches their outstanding business success so that they feel confident and excited to get out from behind the computer and Be Seen!

They realize the high cost of not Being Seen - for example, they aren't using video to market their biz because they are feeling "too fat for the camera" - they are Hiding Behind The Fat, and the computer! These smart, successful women feel an urgent desire for a body that matches what they've already achieved in their business so that they can go to the next level…in their business, and their life…and do it all without that endless struggle with food and their weight.

Because they ARE such smart and fabulously successful women, they feel even more frustrated that they have not been able to solve their food and weight challenges permanently on their own. They often ask themselves, "Since I'm so smart and successful with my biz, why can't I get this weight issue under control?!" The truth is, it's not their fault: none of us can see past our own blind spots, which is why all Olympic athletes and high-achievers have a mindset mentor.

JoLynn empowers and mentors her clients through her step-by-step proven System to permanent weight loss and maintenance to become an Inner Match to the body they desire on the outside. Once you become the YOU on the inside that matches the body (and the life!) you desire on the outside, then it's easy to take the necessary actions to achieve permanent weight loss.

JoLynn is passionate about her work because she knows exactly what it feels like to be stuck in frustration and struggle with your weight and turn to food in an attempt to soothe the fears of really going for it in your business…or any other area of your life. She also knows the joy of releasing those fears and the fat after going from a size 12 to an 8 in only 2 months in

2010, maintaining a size 8 all throughout the toughest time of the year (the holiday season) without deprivation, dieting, or struggle, and then maintaining a size 6 since February, 2011.

As a certified Master NLP Practitioner and coach, JoLynn utilizes her Master level NLP skills (along with the powerful foundation of the law of attraction and her own intuitive abilities), to mentor her clients with a combination of practical directness, accountability, and compassion to Stop Hiding Behind The Fat™ - not only with their body, but in all areas of their life, since how they feel about their body goes with them everywhere! They learn exactly how to release their F.A.T. (Fear Attracting Thoughts) so that they can release the physical fat…without struggle!

Once JoLynn's clients are empowered, out of their own way, and feel good in their own skin, then they are able to soar in their business, their relationships, their spiritual connection, and of course…with their body!

To learn more about JoLynn and how YOU can become the YOU you've always known you could be, grab your complimentary subscription to her *Permanent Weight Loss Secrets* ezine by visiting: www.StopHidingBehindTheFat.com/ezine

www.StopHidingBehindTheFat.com

CHAPTER 5

The Business Woman's Power Advantage!
Using Your **Power Advantage** to
Develop a Business with No Shelf Life!

By Glenna M. Griffin

The recovery room was cold and stark. I sat on the gurney shivering slightly as I waited. These thin hospital gowns were not nearly warm enough. Still a little drowsy from the anesthesia, my eyes adjusted to the bright lights. I wondered how much longer.

Two weeks before I never imagined I would be sitting here. Two weeks earlier I was in the midst of preparing for the new semester of classes at the college where I was an instructor. Two weeks earlier I put my 6 year-old on the kindergarten bus for the first time and smiled at the image of him waving from the bus window. Two weeks before I sat in my 2-year old's play circle at daycare singing with her class. Life was a constant juggle it seemed.

Now as I sat and waited for the doctor to share the results of the biopsy of the lump he had just removed, I shuffled through my mind like an iPod playlist the schedule and what needed to be done. I remember thinking, "I don't have time for this!" There are papers to grade, classes to teach, children to pick up from school, family activities to plan and participate in.......this was not a time to be taken out of the loop with a medical issue!

With great compassion, the doctor informed me I had an advanced stage of an aggressive form of breast cancer. The recommendation for a double mastectomy, chemotherapy, reconstruction and a complete hysterectomy followed. I sat, listened, and tried to process.

I realize now my thoughts turned to one of execution. My mind immediately went into 'strategy' mode. What needed to be done when. It also went into 'change' mode. There would be many changes ahead as specific steps needed to be taken toward treatment and recovery. Finally, it settled on 'resource' mode as I took out my notebook to write down who needed to be contacted, resources I needed to gather, medical appointments I needed to schedule, caretakers I needed to arrange for the children, the list was endless. Around all of this, I remembered that on the way home I needed to pick up the supplies for a birthday cake. I had promised my children I'd help them make a cake to celebrate my 33rd birthday the very next day.

To survive mentally, I pushed the emotions of being diagnosed with cancer and facing my own mortality to one side so I could focus on the physical aspect of eradicating the cancer from my body.

Looking back through the pages of my notebook now I realize I approached the entire treatment plan as a series of business appointments. It became the 'business of survival' and now my business approach is 'survival and longevity.'

According to a recent study, women-owned businesses have grown at nearly twice the rate of all firms! This says something about a woman's **power advantage**. A woman's ability to re-invent, re-generate, and re-vitalize herself whenever a situation arises is natural! These are all components of what make us natural business leaders. These are the components that make us natural creators of *businesses with no shelf life*!

A *business with no shelf life* is a business with no 'expiration date'.

It re-invents, re-designs, re-generates and revitalizes to stay current, focused and successful!

I understand now that one's ability to implement Vision, Strategy and Execution were critical to my success! Within Vision, Strategy and Execution, are the **skills** of change management, strategic management and resource management. These skills carried me through the business of survival those many years ago. These skills are part of a woman's instinctive abilities to succeed in business. We juggle the various components of our lives simultaneously, not always with ease and grace, but with a focus to get the task done!

The **power advantage** is the natural mindset of a woman! The **power advantage** incorporates Vision, Strategy and Execution. It is instinctive to a woman. The benefit of the **power advantage** is a business with no shelf life and success in our personal lives.

I have been focused on creating the very same business with no shelf life. We strive to reach our goal of giving a million people their 'voice', touch five continents within five years, and help people create and live lives of intentional legacy! The long-term result is creating purpose-driven entrepreneurs.

The **power advantage** can be applied by everyone! One way we encourage women to use the **power advantage** is through our philosophy of 'Business with No Shelf Life'! The three core concepts behind the **power advantage** are:

VISION: Women are naturals at looking at the long-term goals. When our children are born and we cradle them in our arms we look out to the future and see the years to come! As women in the workplace, business owners, or entrepreneurs, we look to the long-term goals for what we want to see occur and how we envision our success.

Once the vision is clear, women implement skills of strategic and resource management to make sure we get the job done! The other critical component in creating our vision is *trust*. Without trust we will never accomplish our vision. People buy from people they trust. With our customers and clients, colleagues and children, trust is essential. Create an environment of trust and your business will soar!

WHAT IS YOUR BUSINESS VISION?

STRATEGY: Once the vision is clear, we strategize on how to get to where we want to be. It's no different than walking through the house and picking things up along the way and depositing them where they belong on our way to another room. Women are naturals at strategizing the non-duplication of effort and maximizing our energy!

In the workplace we strategize with our resource management skills, determining as we work through projects and deadlines what is needed and how to obtain those resources.

As we strategize we build *relationships*. Strong relationships allow us to communicate clearly as we learn how the other person (or business) operates. If something needs to be modified or adjusted, the relationship we have with the other party allows us to do so.

WHAT IS YOUR STRATEGY FOR BUSINESS SUCCESS?

EXECUTION: Implementation (or execution) is key to every personal or business goal. To create a business with no shelf life, we must implement the steps needed to work towards the ultimate vision. Taking the first step is fantastic! Following it through to completion is true success!

If we create an environment of *engagement* with our business partners, clients and customers, we are in constant communication to address their needs, goals and concerns. As we work in our businesses, oftentimes changes occur. It might be a change in a deadline, resources, or personnel. Engagement allows us to not be caught off-guard with a situation as we are constantly connected with our listener.

WHAT IS YOUR BUSINESS EXECUTION/IMPLEMENTATION PLAN?

When faced with breast cancer at the age of 33, with two young children and a career just beginning to accelerate, I had two choices. Choice number one was to go into 'retreat mode'. Choice number two was to go to 'survival mode'. This was the path I took. I implemented the concepts of vision, strategy and execution to a situation regarding my health and continued to apply the same concepts to my business success!

I additionally have come to understand to an even higher level that **"people do not care how much you know unless they know how much you care."** A medical environment makes this truly stand out! It makes all the difference in the world. It will make a difference in your business.

This same philosophy carries over easily for women in the workplace. Women are natural nurturers. We have been told that sometimes we show how much we care to a fault and we have to be more 'business-like'. Really? Is it a fault? *I believe a woman's sense of commitment and compassion is what makes us stand out in business!* We're caring! We are focused! We have the ability to adjust and adapt with flexibility!

As a young girl, I can remember sitting at my grandmother's kitchen table and watching her as she worked around the kitchen making a meal. My Grandma was a wonder to watch as she whipped up a meal for a handful or a household full of people! Even in the lean times when there were few things to make a meal from as the cupboards were more bare than full, she managed. She would take a 'little of this' and a 'little of that'.....she'd 'make do' with this and 'make up' that......it was like watching a magic show! She never complained about not having 'just the right thing' but rather would make 'just the right thing' with what she had to work with!

My grandmother never finished high school. She left school to stay at home and help her mother with the family of 10 children. Despite her educational limitations, my grandmother was an instinctive management expert!

Grandma practiced **Resource Management** expertly as she would use whatever resources available to succeed at the goal at hand. As my grandfather worked in the city in the automotive factories, Grandma managed resources and schedules daily as she would have to plan how to coordinate the crops being planted and harvested, daily life on the farm, planning for the cold lean winter months, cycles of seasons and all of the long range planning that goes on when running a farm. Grandma understood and was instinctively practicing forecasting and analysis! In the era that she lived, from the Great Depression and through to 2005, Grandma demonstrated her understanding and expert skill at **Change Management**. She lived through one of the greatest eras of change in our country.....economic and social changes.....she adapted and adjusted constantly! Grandma used her instinctive business mind-set to plan, coordinate, execute the task at hand, and succeed! She created the vision, developed the strategy and performed the execution to meet the goal - survive!

Through the generations, women have succeeded at businesses while juggling other commitments - it's part of our instinct and drive!

Women practice *strategic management* when we start an at-home business to survive financially if we are a caretaker of a parent or caring for our children. We strategize around schedules of others, commitments, a child home sick from school, an appointment that can't be missed....the list is endless! Innovative women entrepreneurs create at-home businesses and juggle the strategy for their success with a balancing act of family and work commitments.

Women practice *resource management* instinctively whether it be in the job place faced with a task at hand and limited resources or at home facilitating the needs of a family! I have spoken with countless women who are managing teams in the workplace and are having to 'make do' while there may be hiring freezes or cuts in spending for resources. Not unlike my grandmother in the kitchen, these professional women are 'making do' with the resources available to them to still succeed at getting the job done! If a new mother chooses to stay home or work part time after the birth of a child, they instinctively figure out how to 'make do' with limited resources so that they can facilitate the desired lifestyle for their child(ren). Woman practice resource management naturally! Eleanor Roosevelt summed it up nicely when she said, "As for accomplishments, I just did what I had to do as things came along."

Change management is another skill instinctive to women. While the world is constantly changing around us, our business and personal lives are constantly growing, changing, developing, and adapting too! If we are unable to change and adapt, we will not survive.

I believe women have a natural courage inside.....a barometer of sorts that determines what we need to handle situations and circumstances. I love the quote "A woman is like a tea bag - you can't tell how strong she is until you put her in hot water."

After almost 20 years in a relationship that was unhealthy, I remember making the choice to make a change. At the time with young children, a new job in a new state, and limited financial means, it was not an easy choice as there were many unknowns. What I did know however was that living in a situation that was not healthy was not serving my children long-term.

As the process of the dis-entanglement of two lives continued, the situation continued to levels that could not have been predicted. I found myself suddenly providing for two children completely on my own and trying to navigate the court systems feeling like I was in a row boat on the open sea. These were changes I could not have anticipated, but like the cancer diagnosis so many years ago, I had to focus on doing what needed to be done to get through. *Change Management* immediately went into practice! I became the 'tea bag' and came to realize how strong I truly was! I became aware that as changes needed to be made and steps taken simply to survive, I was stronger than I realized. The process taught me even greater 'survival mode' techniques which I continue to incorporate into my business.

Oprah Winfrey said, "Follow your instincts. That's where true wisdom manifests itself." I believe as women we truly have the instincts that allow us to excel at business! We have the power to create meaningful and successful personal and professional lives! True wisdom to guide our next steps comes from following our instincts to create personal lives of passion and success and business lives with no-shelf life! We are natural re-inventors!

Women have the ability through the **power advantage** to truly create **businesses with no shelf life**! Woman are able to adapt, collaborate, strategize, discover, analyze, and make choices that propel them to unanticipated heights! When I think of my grandmother and the management skills she instinctively depended on, when I think of the millions of women who re-invent themselves after business changes, life changes, illnesses, family decisions.......women are natural change agents!

Women have the **POWER ADVANTAGE**!

The United Nations dubbed 1975 as the 'Year of the Woman' and proclaimed it's theme song as Helen Reddy's song "I am Woman Hear Me Roar!' In these economic times of challenge and opportunity, with woman-owned businesses growing stronger than ever, it is time to make THIS year YOUR year for personal greatness and professional success!

Be a woman who means business. Use the **power advantage**! Make your business a business with no shelf life!

We dare you!

For more information on this and other topics, contact Glenna at: glenna@speakamerica.com.

About Glenna

Glenna M. Griffin, Remarkability Expert
COO, Speak America
Co-Founder, Let Your Life Speak Foundation

Glenna Griffin is driven to encourage others to make positive choices and changes in their lives! The power of choice and the power of change can result in outstanding personal and professional success!

As seen in USA Today and in the Wall Street Journal, on FOX, CBS, NBC and ABC, Glenna is a sought after speaker and trainer. Speak America is a national resource organization for remarkability, dedicated to helping people create and live lives of 'Intentional Legacy.' Through personal and professional experience, Glenna encourages the development of personal communication skills for the discovery of an individual's true "voice." When someone finds their voice and purpose, and has the ability to share that discovery with others, the world truly benefits from the gift.

As co-founder of the Let Your Life Speak Foundation, Glenna travels the world sharing her communication gifts.

Author of *YES YOU CAN! - Reaching Your Potential While Achieving Greatness*, *GPS FOR SUCCESS - Goals And Proven Strategies From The Industry's Leading Experts*, *WIN - 35 Winning Strategies From Today's Leading Entrepreneurs*, and *BIG IDEAS FOR YOUR BUSINESS*, Glenna is available for guest appearances at conferences or to lead group seminars.

Contact Glenna directly at: glenna@speakamerica.com or 866-609-2333.

CHAPTER 6

22 Lessons From The Top

By Cheryl L. Clarkson

A business maven's reflection on 35 years in business and the characteristics needed at each level in the climb to the top.

My career is not nearly over yet; if anything I have another 35 years of maven-dom ahead of me. I love the business of business.

However, I have now entered that stage of life where my new employees will slip and make a comment such as, "Oh, you're the same age as my mother!" The first time I was told that I was the same age as the parents of one of my younger employees, I was stunned into silence as I did the mental math. That employee is now happily working at Dairy Queen (just kidding), but it got me to thinking….

I started to reflect on my career to date. I am more comfortable looking forward than behind, but my curiosity started getting the better of me. How WAS it that I have been able to move so far ahead in business? I knew it was more than flat-out hard work, though I am certainly a workaholic. I knew it wasn't just luck, even though we all need a healthy dose of that. My conclusion was that there was a handful of traits or skills that had been necessary to master, which then allowed me to get the next promotion, the next rung on the ladder.

My career began as a Sales Representative for a division of a Fortune 500 Company in the business of medical and hospital supplies. My job, specifically, was to call on all the hospitals in the state of Arizona, and convince them to buy their food service and nutritional supplies from my company. I covered 113,998 square miles of turf, including clinics on Native American reservations, and drove from hospital to hospital with, yes, a clothes rod suspended from the ceiling in the backseat of my car to hold my clothes. The dress code in those days was IBM-type grey pinstripe skirt suits, white collared shirts, and "girl ties", little silk bow tie thingamajigs in Brooks Brothers prints.

I convinced enough hospital administrators to upgrade to our products that I was launched into management. Thus began an upward career spiral that brought me many new challenges and opportunities in mid-level, then upper- level management, and ultimately the opportunity to run entire corporations.

So how did I go from my first job of selling hospital dietary supplies to sitting on Boards of Directors of NASDAQ companies? Based on my personal experience, there are certain traits and learned skills that are important at each stage of a career path. Those skills are carried into the next position, and we keep adding layers of learned traits. As we progress in our careers this acquired skill set becomes ingrained.

For starters, there are certain core criteria that must be met to be successful at any stage of a career ladder. It is assumed that one will:

- Meet and exceed assigned goals and expectations
- Maintain a positive attitude
- Shower regularly and practice good personal hygiene
- Refrain from posting nude photographs of oneself on the internet

Once you've met those conditions, you're ready for the rest. So, let's get on with it; here's my list of 22 Lessons From the Top.

AS AN EMPLOYEE

1. Work hard, work long, be visible (for modern-day ambitious folks; don't work from home if an office option is available)

2. Practice makes perfect, be relentless at mastering your job responsibilities

3. Be loyal to your business unit, your immediate boss, and your bosses' boss

4. Take on additional tasks or projects that others may shirk, especially if by doing so it will make your boss's life easier.

AS A MANAGER (at all levels)

5. Earn the respect of your direct reports. If you don't, they can, and will, sabotage you.

6. Be honest, be fair, be consistent

7. Be humble, give most of the credit to your team

8. Surround yourself with results-orientated team members

AS A CEO

9. Trust your gut when it comes to people and situations.

10. Be bold, but not reckless.

11. Hone your public speaking skills. You must be an effective communicator and be comfortable in the spotlight.

12. Keep yourself in top physical shape and maintain your wardrobe and grooming. Results will keep you in your job, but image does count at this level. Find a great tailor and spend some serious money on shoes.

AS AN ENTREPRENEUR / BUSINESS OWNER

14. Resilience. You may have a lot of bad days, scary days, do-we-have-enough-cash-to-meet-payroll days. As the song says, pick yourself up, brush yourself off and start all over again. And again. And again. And again…

15. Originality; thinking out of the box. If you are an entrepreneur, chances are nobody has done what you are doing or the way you are doing it. You are one of a kind, baby! Figure out a way to unforgettably differentiate your product or service.

16. Passion for a cause. I left the corporate world 14 years ago to found my company after a personal tragedy. My sister, who was my only sibling and my best friend, died of malignant melanoma a few days after her 40th birthday. From that time on, I have devoted my life to preventing others from dying from this relentless cancer.

AS A BUSINESS MAVEN

There are many terms and titles that could be substituted here. I am using the term to mean senior business leadership and wisdom, which also encompasses outside business interests, board work, smaller ventures, etc.

17. Guard the brand and be the brand.

A good brand identity takes years to hone and nurture. Once it is established, you can tweak it, but jealously guard it. The brand message must be consistent throughout the organization.

As the leader of your organization, you personify the brand. You must be consistent with the values of the brand. Your employees also represent the brand. For example, at my company, our brand stands for sun safety and protection. Therefore, our employees don't bake in the sun or become overly tan. That would be a slap in the face to our brand.

Our brand stands for health. During our interviews we are candid about the fact that we don't hire employees who smoke. That may seem harsh, but that would not be consistent with our brand and our values.

Our brand stands for personalized service. We don't use an automated phone system. We answer our phones the old-fashioned way, by one of our smiling employees asking, "How may I assist you?"

18. Stay flexible on work/family balance issues.

Flexibility is critical to keeping and motivating working mothers and fathers. That doesn't mean giving them time off at the expense of the Company and other co-workers. It does mean on a case-by-case basis, allowing four-day workweeks, part-time employment, job sharing, and not raising eyebrows when employees attend school plays, teacher conferences and big games.

It also means setting expectations that they have a back-up plan in place for when their child is sick or it is school vacation week. The needs of the business still have to come first, but creating a flexible work environment can pay dividends in employee loyalty, and productivity.

19. Adhere to a "No drama" policy.

People often ask me about what it is like managing a mostly female staff, and I can tell by the expectant look on their faces or their tone of voice, as if they are saying "Tell me the dirt." There is no dirt. Our team has no tolerance for DRAMA. That is not to say that if an employee has a true crisis: a sick child, disloyal spouse or car accident, that it should be brushed under the rug. It does mean that a professional demeanor is required at all times when on the job.

If an employee needs time off or needs to talk about a true crisis, that's fine. However, chronic drama is a no-no, defined as: gossip, snarkiness, pettiness, spats, overt self-pity, cattiness or passive-aggressive behavior. It is simply not accepted, and if an employee exhibits any of those characteristics, we have made a hiring miscalculation and we need to sever the relationship.

20. Hire only people you like on a personal level.

At this stage of my career, I have no tolerance for working with people who are not a perfect fit with our company. If I don't like them, chances are our clients wouldn't like them. Once qualified candidates have passed all the interviews, vetting and screening, before I make a final decision to hire, they have to pass the dinner table test, which is: would I enjoy having them to my home for dinner? Would I enjoy their company sitting around our dinner table, interacting with my husband and children? Would my husband think he or she was boring? Would my son think he or she is a phoney? Would my daughter think they were loud or pretentious? I call it the dinner table test.

A disclaimer: this is a *virtual* test; I would not subject these poor souls to the actual experience. It is a mind exercise.

21. Sweat the small stuff if it affects your core competencies.

Being mired in details when you are leading an organization is not a good practice. However, some hands-on management from the top can be beneficial to ensure the success of the Company's core competencies.

One of our company's core competencies is providing

excellent sunscreens to help prevent skin cancer. We don't create sunscreens that are "good enough." We create sunscreens that are the best in the world. Certain aspects of this process are delegated, but I am ever-present in every detail of sunscreen decision-making for the ingredients, labeling, advertising, marketing channels, etc. I am also relentless at making sure we educate our employees, our clients, and the world, … about how to select an effective sunscreen.

22. Take a deep breath; slow down decision-making.

This is a challenge for me. I didn't get to where I am by being inherently patient. However, patience is one of the keys to my success at this level. It could be the fact that I have matured. It could be a characteristic we all develop as we age. All I know is I have learned to take a few deep breaths and keep things in perspective much better than I did earlier in my career.

The problem is, my quick decisions and quick reactions are often right. The other problem is, sometimes they're not, with less than desirable consequences and hurt feelings. Especially in this day of instant communications -- email and texts -- I've learned it's a best to pause, take a deep breath and think through the wording of my decisions and responses.

All of the above traits are important, and in my growth as a leader, I am always looking for better ways to do things and areas for improvement. A career is a journey and there are new challenges every day. Business is hard. Managing people is hard. *The challenge is what makes success, when it comes, all the more rewarding!*

About Cheryl

Cheryl L. Clarkson is the Founder and CEO of Skin-Health™, Inc. in Boston, MA. SkinHealth owns and operates three medical spas which offer advanced skin care, laser and cosmetic surgery procedures, and two retail stores featuring the SkinHealth™ line of cosmeceutical skin care products.

The medical spas are affiliated with the area's most respected cosmetic surgeons and dermatologists. The highly acclaimed SkinHealth product line won the coveted Health Magazine award for Best Sunscreen and was selected for inclusion in the Screen Actors' Guild (SAG) celebrity gift baskets. The products have been featured in Vanity Fair, Town and Country, Cosmopolitan, Glamour and Health Magazines.

Cheryl holds a Masters of Science degree in business from the Sloan School of Management at the Massachusetts Institute of Technology.

At 39 years of age, Ms. Clarkson became one of the youngest women ever to be named CEO of a publicly-traded NASDAQ company. She has served as President of four highly-respected medical device and medical services companies.

In addition, Ms. Clarkson has served on the Board of Directors of five highly-respected corporations, two of which were publicly traded and two of which were sold to large, publicly traded corporations. She has been appointed Lead Director, Chairman of the Compensation Committee, and has served on Audit and Nominating Committees on these corporate boards.

She has been featured on NBC news on skin care and skin cancer prevention, Fox News affiliates on the prevention and rejuvenation of aging skin, and was featured in Fortune Magazine as a skin care expert. She writes a beauty advice column, "Ask Cheryl" for several magazines and a blog of the same name.

To learn how to "Look Fresh and Vibrant at Any Age" with the SkinHealth product line, you can visit www.shopskinhealth.com or call 877-705-SKIN (7546).

CHAPTER 7

Ten Daily Habits of a Leader

By Nancy J. Geenen, MA Ed., JD

Business success is the direct result of making decisions and taking action at all levels of an enterprise. Mission statements and strategic plans articulate the vision and ignite the heart, but do not dictate the daily action required for success. Great leaders use the vision to inspire talented colleagues to do one thing: create value for clients. Profits, not just revenues, flow when inspired colleagues perform challenging work for clients who feel the value of the relationship. Leaders develop these traits in others by listening actively and inspiring action.

All good; but what do I do every day?

As a newly appointed office-managing partner of a national firm, I found myself without any business training. I had been a successful trial lawyer for many years and occupied a handful of leadership roles throughout my career. I knew how to inspire a team to success. Yet, trial teams focus on a single goal with strategies that are solely geared to win. I was unprepared for the challenges of leading the infrastructure that supported 60 lawyers in multiple offices operating as part of a 500+ lawyer firm. Talk about herding cats! I read business books and talked to law firm leaders, both within and outside my organization. All expressed their condolences, and most offered advice that was too generic to be helpful. I was already into the second quarter of the fiscal year and budget estimates predicted a half-million dollar loss. The firm's leadership wanted measurable results. What to do? Where to start?

The first week after my "promotion", I asked the firm's managing partner to define success for me. I learned about the firm's financial model and the metrics that make a law firm profitable. I learned that I had wide latitude to manage as long as I improved the metrics over a reasonable period of time.

I started with the skills I knew. I worked the assignment like I work a new case. I sat myself in a conference room and had each of the local department leaders teach me about the system. I asked only one question: how would you redesign the system to make it more valuable to the client? There were no interruptions. I watched not only the presentations, but also the manner by which the team presented the information. I paid attention to whether the managers talked about clients, results, process, or other managers. I noted whether the managers spoke from the head, heart or pocketbook. I catalogued the responses.

Clearly in a turnaround scenario, we rebuilt and streamlined local systems to do everything about a few things, rather than a few things about everything. I focused the leadership team on two core values: working smarter (largely internal tasks) and improving client service (largely external tasks). We developed a strategy that everyone could remember, repeat on a daily basis, and use to re-examine the purpose of the work. I engaged in daily tasks that focused on building an innovative work environment. Over the years, I streamlined these tasks into ten daily habits on which I rely for success.

- Scan News and Industry Headlines
- Review the Company Dashboard and Website
- Prioritize Task Lists and Clear Messages

- Walkabout the Company
- Think about Ideas, Ingenuity, and Innovation
- Focus on Business Development, Marketing, or Public Relations
- Take Care of a Client
- Learn and Reflect
- Train and Inspire
- Celebrate and Promote Success

These Ten Daily Habits capitalize on both an internal and external scan of my working environment and the company's success metrics.

1. NEWS AND INDUSTRY HEADLINES

Reading the news should always be the first task of the day and is a different activity than listening to a morning news show. I subscribe to the weekend New York Times and thus receive the digital "Times Digest" daily. I scan the headlines and read two to three articles that catch my attention. This digital read replaces a clipping service that prepared regional, industry, and financial news for my daily scan. I also use aggregator feeds that focus on small business topics. Alltop and AmEx Open are two of my favorites to get industry and small business news. The danger here is trying to read too much information, including blogs, Twitter, Facebook and LinkedIn group updates. I delegate the sifting to others on the executive team and/or my assistant. I focus on high level trends and policy events that affect my industry and on those items that are of personal interest.

2. COMPANY DASHBOARD AND WEBSITE

Each time I log in to my system, I see the company dashboard – in fact, I use tidbits from this summary during my "walkabout." The dashboard is a visual representation of the performance indicators that are important to the growth of the company. In order to get meaningful metrics, the IT team must have a working understanding of our success metrics. As an early adopter of technology, I communicate regularly with the IT team to understand the capabilities of the system and to develop an innovative dashboard of performance indicators and reports. Over time, we devise a working and useful system. The daily review of these indicators allows me to compare my strategy and action plan to actual performance. I only take time for analysis and questions if I see an outlier or new trend emerging.

I also review the company website and the websites of two market competitors through the eyes of a client. I often find news or other information that might not make it to my desk. Sometimes, I get to celebrate, but I am always reminded of the different value propositions. And, I often find fun facts to share and questions to ask during my walkabout.

3. TASK LIST, CALENDAR, EMAIL AND VOICEMAIL

This is perhaps the most tedious and cumbersome activity of my Daily Habits and can take up much of my morning if not actively managed. However, these actions are key communication opportunities. The task list is not a project list. Projects are delegated to the leadership team. The task list is not longer than the three to five items that I will accomplish by the end each day. I get great joy and satisfaction as I cross an item off my list. Using both an electronic and paper system, I revise and commit to my schedule and tasks, which sets the course for my day.

Along with tasks and calendaring, I review and clear

my email and voicemail messages each morning. Internally, I have established acceptable email and voicemail behavior that leads to effective and efficient use of the technology available to the company. My assistant has full access to my email and voicemail. I do not read email messages that are longer than a few lines. I do not listen to voicemail messages that are longer than thirty seconds. An effective assistant will filter and prioritize messages so that there are only two tasks: respond or delegate for a response. One caveat to this Daily Habit: it is crucial to appear approachable. Unanswered calls, e-mails or notes will elicit comments no leader should ever hear: "I thought you were too busy;" or, "You can't possibly be interested in what I'm doing." I want my colleagues to know that I respect the passion required for great work. I treat my colleagues like I treat my most important client.

4. WALKABOUT

After completing the first three Daily Habits, it is time to get out of the "executive" chair and walkabout the company. I have plenty of material with which to start a conversation or acknowledge a work group. I take time to listen to the "local" news. This is both a physical and an electronic activity. The walk allows me to touch every person. And, I do mean touch. A hand on a shoulder with a personal remark is an effective way to take notice and inspire. The walkabout takes me through the reception area, into the communal areas, around the bullpen, and into the service area. In virtual companies or those with multiple offices, this walkabout is achieved through the effective use of technology. Skype and Go-to-Meeting are just two services that are free or relatively inexpensive. I also make a point to be in each office at least three days a month so that I reach every employee. Once again, I have no agenda. My message is simple: I am available. Action, not words, inspire.

5. IDEAS, INGENUITY AND INNOVATION

This Daily Habit is time spent thinking about big ideas: re-imagining the process, comparing performance to key goals, and identifying the actions that limit growth. Ingenuity is the willingness to act beyond current limitations and boundaries. Innovation is the courage to embrace change without clinging to the safety of the status quo. It is my job to define successful growth and draw correlations between growth and the team's activity. This is thinking time for me to examine the pathways to success: what's working and what's not. Every milestone is important. This Habit, like getting to the gym, requires discipline: to truly take the time to just sit and think – and it looks different to every leader. Sweat when necessary, but take time to sit with a quiet mind. I use a quote attributed to Indira Gandhi for inspiration: "Be still in the midst of chaos and vibrantly alive in repose."

6. BUSINESS DEVELOPMENT/MARKETING/ PUBLIC RELATIONS

I like focusing on these areas after I spend time thinking about innovation and new ideas. I have more energy and enthusiasm for an activity that requires movement and action. I rotate one activity in each area for each day of the week as part of my daily task list. A week of activities might include a morning phone call to a warm lead; a lunch with a media contact; a first-hand review of our company swag and tchotchkes for an upcoming conference; prospecting and researching a company that might need our services; and attending the bi-weekly meeting of our lead business developers. Business development, marketing, and public relations are areas so vast and deep that I never lack for an activity. Many weeks, my days are already scheduled with meals, receptions, or conferences that I count toward this Daily Habit.

7. CLIENT CARE

Each day, I call, visit, or Skype with a client to develop and nurture a personal relationship unrelated to any sales call. I like to find out how we are doing from the client's perspective. I am focused on the client buying experience (the feeling), not the quality of our product. I schedule an appointment in advance The client relationship manager provides me with the latest news about the client, our successes and our failures. Generally, I meet with the company owner, but other senior managers and decision makers might attend as well. Such meetings may last fifteen minutes or two hours, depending on the medium and time of day. I like face-to-face meetings best, but proximity may make such events problematic. Again, I listen actively and do not worry about having answers or solutions. At the conclusion of the meeting, I ask what I can do for the client. I always come away with new insights, new work, and a better relationship. An important aspect of this Daily Habit is to disseminate the feedback to the rest of the leadership team. Sharing client feedback on a daily basis teaches the leadership team to adapt and respond in a client focused work environment.

8. LEARN AND REFLECT

The practice of this Daily Habit is reflective and introspective. Generally, it is an early afternoon activity and focused on right brain thinking. I might read an article about an outlier, have coffee with an artist friend, watch a TED video, talk to a peer leader in another industry, or take Spanish lessons. My goal is to enhance my ability to create, adapt, and respond to an ever-changing market place. I want to learn something new or think about something old in a new way. I work to free myself from the fear and small-mindedness that inhibits or prohibits growth. Practicing this Habit takes immense confidence and courage. This is not a time to procrastinate; it is scheduled time to explore.

9. TRAIN AND INSPIRE

The return on time spent with the company superstars is priceless. In an unmanaged day, a leader is consumed with problems and managing solutions. Using an 80-20 rule for training and mentoring, I spend 80 percent of the time with my top performers. I let the HR leaders manage problem employees. I choose one performer each day and spend ten to thirty minutes in a one-on-one discussion about mastery, meaning and autonomy. We focus our discussion on transforming challenges, whether personal or professional, into a passion for excellence. I want every person in the company to anticipate and solve client issues and to adapt to the ever changing needs of the working environment. I strive to create a work environment inspired by love where colleagues feel heroic in their daily actions.

10. CELEBRATE

Over time, the practice of these Ten Daily Habits produces tangible and intangible results. Publicly celebrate the small wins without delay; do not wait for the end of the week or end of the month. Daily recognition fuels continued dedication to the greater mission of the team. Promote success about clients as well as team members. Acknowledge the process, just as much as the final result. This is an opportunity for leadership to connect with the "doers" among a team: those deserving individuals, who not only "get it done," but set the standards for excellence. This notion of celebrating ultimately recommits a team to sustainable success and to the leader who cleared the way.

These Ten Daily Habits keep me focused on the "right stuff." At first, it was a struggle to stick to this schedule. I limited the time I spent on the internally focused habits (reading news, clearing task lists, calendar, and messages, and big thinking) to twenty minutes each. And, there was never enough time to complete the task at hand. That said, with each passing week, I became more proficient and effective so that I no longer was driven by time, but solely by the task. I had time to think about activities that would transform the company. The leader's "job" is to keep the company doing more of what it does best, and less of everything else. This daily focus transforms good intentions and hope for success into actionable, practical and realistic "to do" items that anchor whole teams to a singular purpose amidst a sea of distraction. Practicing the Ten Daily Habits creates time and space for a leader to experience the *tabula rasa* moments of inspiration that clear the way for success.

About Nancy

 Nancy J. Geenen, MA Ed., JD, is a Founder and the Managing Director of Suann Ingle Communications, a member of the CompassLys Group.

Suann Ingle Communications helps attorneys and executives deliver great presentations, integrating the principles of graphic design, focus group and jury research, purposeful communication techniques, and interactive presentation technology to achieve consistent and effective presentations in the courtroom or the boardroom. Nancy formulates strategy and trains her clients in presentation and communication skills. As a practicing lawyer, Nancy has tried or arbitrated over 150 business disputes, including commercial, financial, and intellectual property cases. She counsels clients on risk assessment and litigation management, consults with trial teams in bench and jury trials, settlement, mediation, and arbitration, and offers trial skills training to law firms.

In 1998 and 1999, Nancy worked in Geneva, Switzerland for the United Nations Compensation Commission as team leader and senior legal officer. While working at the UN, she investigated and prosecuted over $10 billion in contract claims and other business injuries filed by 420 business entities from 45 countries and incurred as a result of the 1990 Gulf War. Nancy was named a Northern California SuperLawyer in business and intellectual property litigation from 2004 through 2010.

In 2010, Nancy was elected to the inaugural class of the Forever Influential Business Women Hall of Fame by The San Francisco Business Times. During her three terms as Managing Partner for the Northern California offices of Foley & Lardner LLP, Nancy joined the list of Most Influential Business Women in the Bay Area for six consecutive years. She also served three terms on the Board of Directors of the San Francisco Chamber of Commerce with two consecutive terms as an at-large member of the Executive Committee. A current member of the Women's President Organization, she served one year on its Board of Directors.

With over 25 years of legal and management experience in the United States and Europe, Nancy speaks and writes frequently on leadership, risk analysis, and jury trial presentation. Her recent articles and presentations include: Business Development for Attorneys: *Using Trial Consultants with End Clients,* The Jury Expert, The American Association of Trial Consultants, January 2012; *Eureka! Moments on the Path to Successful Visual Presentations in the Courtroom,* The Jury Expert, The American Association of Trial Consultants, September 2011; *Networking: Breaking the Glass Ceiling,* SF Bar Association, January 2010; *Foundations for Developing and Implementing Strategic Plans,* UC Hastings College of Law, Leadership Academy for Women, July 2010; *Women Leading Law Firms,* Law Practice and Management, Bar Association of San Francisco, January 2010; *Managing Partner Q&A,* Law Practice Magazine, December 2008; *Taking Risks, Making Decisions, & Other Challenges of Women Law Firm Leaders,* UC Hastings College of Law, Leadership Academy for Women, July 2008; Effective Mentoring of Women Attorneys, Retaining & Developing Women Lawyers, ACI, December 2007; *Club v. Business, Managing the Evolving Law Firm,* American Legal Administrators, National Conference, 2005; *Beating the Odds: Success Strategies for Creating Gender Equity in the Legal Profession,* State Bar Association of California, 2004; *Developing Law Firm Leaders,* Edge International, 2003; *Courtroom Psychology and Trial Advocacy,* Richard Waites (2003), contributing writer on Opening Statements.

CHAPTER 8

Core Values Can Take You To The Next Level

By Jena Gardner

September of 2009 was not a time to be optimistic in business, but I had no other choice. JG Black Book of Travel, a company I had founded eight years before, had just made *Inc.* magazine's list of the fastest-growing private businesses in America. I left New York for the magazine's annual conference in DC feeling quietly confident.

JG Black Book had grown from a one-person representation firm into one of the travel industry's leading names in sales and marketing. Even in the midst of a recession, through all of the challenges we and so many other businesses faced, we had managed to grow, to add new staff and new clients. We had done well for ourselves and I was enormously proud of my team and our success.

Still, I was becoming restless. The desire for something greater, both for my business and for myself, made me want to push further. I sensed that I had arrived at the start of something new and unfamiliar and I wanted us to thrive, not just survive, in the new realities of the market in which we found ourselves.

And so I went to the Inc. conference looking for some answers. I imagine that like many of the other entrepreneurs in attendance, I had come with the hope of discovering some magic formula that would help transform my company into a billion dollar business (or at least land us a spot on The Oprah Winfrey Show). The thought of us churning our wheels for another five years and sticking to the same strategic script was no longer acceptable to me. I had reached a point of understanding that it was time to take our efforts to the next level but was unsure of how exactly that change would come about.

Luckily for me the conference's keynote speaker was a man who knew intimately what it took to do just that. But instead of sharing with us that insider secret, Jim Collins – noted author and one of my favorite minds in business – asked how many of us in the audience had written down our core values. Out of a sea of hundreds, maybe 10 people raised their hands. Sure I felt better knowing I wasn't the only one that had skipped out on that assignment but over and over again he returned to the same questions: *What is the greater purpose of your work? What does your company believe in? What are your core values?*

To be honest I had never put much thought into defining JG Black Book's core values before that point. When you start a company or own a small business I think you tend to assume that everyone understands why they're there and what the organization's purpose is because they know you. The first two people I hired were my aunt and a close friend. After that it was my friends, more family and a few old colleagues. The company had grown so organically that it never seemed necessary to have a formal meeting to discuss what we believed in or what our common vision for the future was – we all just did what we had to do to stay afloat.

As time went on and JG Black Book grew, I naturally became less available. And whether I noticed or not, the values of my company were being shaped not by me or my vision but through the daily interactions my staff had with our clients, our industry partners and each other. Many companies – including my own – run on the assumption that when you hire qualified people, you're all working under the same set of values. In business it seems fundamental to hire people who are hard-working, honest and loyal. The danger comes in assuming that the work ethic of individuals is enough for a company to rely on as it grows.

Unfortunately, we had never taken the time as a group to agree on where we were going or how we wanted to get there. It was left to each of us as individuals to navigate each day and each new challenge on our own. And because of that, because each of us was moving in our own direction, we struggled to move forward as quickly and effectively as I was hoping we could.

Knowing that if the question of core values was on Jim Collins's mind, it should be on mine, I took some time on the train back to New York to scribble down my initial thoughts. I sketched out my own ideas of how I saw (or how I wanted to see) JG Black Book and planned to send my list out to the team the next day.

But then, as often happens, reality got in the way. The phone calls began, emails piled up, meetings came and went and the question of core values fell out of my mind. It seemed as though there were always more pressing issues to attend to and more important priorities on my plate. That may have been the case to this day if not for a few members of my Executive Team who pushed me to revisit that list I had made weeks before.

It's easy as a business owner to be consumed by cash flow and contracting. I was among those who, for a long time, brushed aside the discussion of core values as a 'nice to have' and not a 'need to have'. But after weeks of seeing the same patterns and same issues return, it became clear that nothing would ever change until I prioritized defining our core values.

THE PROCESS

What I thought would be an afternoon affair turned into a six-month process and our company is all the better for it. In that time, we must have gone through 300 ideas and 15 revisions. We held all-team meetings, round table brainstorming sessions and secret ballots. And in the end we came up with a single document that outlined the standard to which we agreed we'd hold ourselves and each other accountable:

(i).   **B**uild lasting and meaningful partnerships.

(ii). **L**augh, be happy and have fun.

(iii). **A**ct in JGBB's best interests at all times.

(iv). **C**reate a community for our team and our partners based on trust, respect and honesty.

(v).   **K**eep at the cutting edge of the industry – lead and innovate.

(vi). **B**e a part of something extraordinary.

(vii). **O**wn your work and deliver outstanding results.

(viii). **O**pen your mind, be adventurous and creative.

(ix). **K**eep alert for problems and identify and address root causes.

They are simple and straightforward but that was the point: to find a common ground upon which we'd build our future success. Not too long into the process, I came to realize that this was of greater importance than the marketing plan we had developed, the development presentations we had created and even the initial business plan I started the company with. This was the basis of everything: it's the foundation of who you are (as a company and as individuals) and what you want to do in life.

It's about finding what energizes you and your staff to go to work every day. It's about knowing the people you work with and understanding that you all share a common purpose. It's about pride and commitment, accountability and, most importantly, community. The community I had built initially, like many first-time entrepreneurs, was one centered on people and personalities. The community we have now created is one based around shared priorities and a common vision. *That* is a much stronger foundation on which to build.

If you looked at our company three years ago, it was so easily definable. We offered a specific service to a specific market, hoping to achieve significant growth by doing the same thing we had always done. Now that we've defined ourselves and our purpose as an organization, it has opened the door for our firm to be so much more flexible, dynamic and creative. New services, new divisions, even entirely new companies have been born from our decision to get serious about defining and living our core values.

To that end, we started a non-profit foundation, The Bodhi Tree Foundation, aimed at motivating our industry to give back to the people and places that make travel so rewarding. We built a public relations division that has since grown to become its own company. And we launched The Traveler's Collection, a retail website featuring clothing, accessories and home décor from artisans around the world. None of that would have been possible if we had kept our focus centered only on the tasks we had right in front of us.

Perspective is an underrated value in business. That ability – to see clearly, to anticipate problems, to envision something bigger for my company – became stronger because of our core values and because of the time spent creating them.

For those thinking about embarking on the process of defining their company culture, I thought I might share a few tips we learned about how to be most effective:

A. Align your team.

Growth is rarely an easy process and there is no one-size-fits-all solution. The process of creating core values will likely be a difficult one for your organization, especially if done the right way. Still, ensuring that your entire team is in line with the company's vision and direction is worth the pains you may encounter. Finding alignment among everyone will make certain your team can keep pace no matter how fast or unexpected growth comes.

In my own experience, different teams or divisions within a company think very differently about what the company is, what its core strengths are and what its path to success will require. Once we decided on the nine values above however, it was imperative to have buy-in from everyone. I asked each person, point blank, whether or not they were 'on the bus', whether they were up for embarking on the course which we had set.

Sure everyone agreed out loud, but in their words and in their actions some began to show that they could not or would not move in the direction we were headed. I sensed, as did my staff, that there were a few team members who lacked the level of commitment to our values and to our purpose that would be required of us moving forward.

If I learned anything from this process it is to not prolong the inevitable. In retrospect, it was more painful for me, for those employees who weren't a good fit and, most importantly, for the team, for those individuals to stay on board with us. I think that as women we have a natural desire to nurture people. That instinct, however, can distract from what we know to be true. In this case, it was evident to everyone involved, including me, who was stalling the growth process. Still, I wanted to believe that I could change how they felt, how they worked, and how they interacted with others. I ultimately learned that that was both beyond my control and beyond my responsibilities.

If I could offer one piece of advice, it would be to make the difficult decisions that are required to assure a positive and united community quickly. It does no one any good to pretend that fundamental differences in goals, priorities and principles do not exist. It was very difficult to see team members leave, but they knew, as did I that we could disagree on strategies and tactics, but at the end of the day we all had to believe in the mission and values of the company in order for it to prosper.

B. Live your values.

We now take time at every one of our quarterly team meetings to revisit our core values. We have integrated them into our annual employee reviews, rewarding those who model the spirit of our company. We introduce the core values during every new hire interview and even bring copies to share with potential clients.

It's not enough to have your core values written down. I felt compelled to lead by those values and to empower my staff to make decisions based on them. Hold your staff accountable to what you agreed on and allow them to take ownership. I was amazed to see how our company grew – in ways I hadn't ever imagined – once everyone was given free rein to work based on values and not on tasks.

To aid in that process, make your values clear, specific and actionable. Simon Sinek, another of my favorite speakers and authors, had this to say about the most successful company cultures:

"For values or guiding principles to be truly effective they have to be verbs. It's not 'integrity,' it's 'always do the right thing.' It's not 'innovation,' it's 'look at the problem from a different angle.' Articulating our values as verbs gives us a clear idea… of how to act in any situation."

C. Be for something bigger.

My company is at its heart a consulting firm servicing the tourism industry. Our purpose, however, as individuals and as a company, is much bigger than that. Collectively we agreed that we wanted:

- To lead the world to inspired destinations.
- To inspire within others a passion for travel at the highest levels of quality and meaningfulness.
- To promote tourism as a means towards a more connected and peaceful world.
- To harness the strength of the global travel industry to preserve the planet's natural and cultural treasures.

While serving the needs of our clients and meeting our revenue targets are still enormously important for us, that mission is what motivates us to get out of bed every morning. While your competitors obsess over tactics to one-up each other, be mindful of your larger mission and purpose as a company. Let your core values guide you and your team through difficult decisions, new market realities and unforeseen challenges. Don't worry about what everyone else is thinking or doing, worry about what you think, what *inspires* you, and others will take notice.

About Jena

Jena Gardner is President and CEO of the Global Group by JG.

Entrepreneur, marketing expert and travel industry veteran, Jena Gardner turned a lifelong passion for travel into a thriving enterprise. Her company, Global Group by JG, is a world-leader with the travel and travel lifestyle industries. Its portfolio of distinctive brands is active across three different sectors: sales and marketing, public relations and retail. Her innovative approach to business has made Ms. Gardner a sought-after industry consultant and speaker. Named one of the Top 25 Most Extraordinary Minds in Sales and Marketing by HSMAI, Ms. Gardner has been invited to speak at such prestigious events as the Global Women's Forum, the Global Eco Conference, the *Fortune* Luxury Summit, the Luxury Marketing Council and the Luxury Portfolio SUMMIT. She is also a contributing writer for *Enterprising Women* magazine.

Ms. Gardner founded JG Black Book of Travel in 2002 and has since built it into a highly successful consulting firm that provides expert sales, marketing and distribution services to the world's finest travel experiences. The firm has been named by Inc. magazine as one of the country's fastest growing privately-held companies for the past three years. Ms. Gardner is also President and CEO of JG Group PR, a New York-based public relations agency and in 2009 she launched The Traveler's Collection, a retail website showcasing exclusive and unique home décor, apparel and accessory items from artisans around the globe.

Knowing the depth and scale of the travel industry's influence, Ms. Gardner continues to work to promote philanthropy, economic development and environmental sustainability through tourism. She is co-founder and president of The Bodhi Tree Foundation, a non-profit organization dedicated to mobilizing travelers and the tourism industry to promote environmental and humanitarian efforts across the globe. Ms. Gardner also serves on the Judging Committee for the World Travel and Tourism Council's Tourism for Tomorrow Awards, which recognizes and promotes best practices in sustainable tourism.

A proud Montana native, Ms. Gardner graduated with honors from the University of Montana's School of Business Administration.

CHAPTER 9

Buy your Own Castle – Don't Wait For The PRINCE!

By Orit Koren

The conference room is lit with the bright blue-green fluorescent glow of sci-fi films and scary hospital rooms while everything seems to be moving in slow motion, frame by frame. The "team" of big wigs from XYZ Bank is all seated around the large oak conference table in their high-backed leather chairs, hands furiously scribbling notes on standard office-issue notepads. You can see them through the glass walls as you approach the room – wishing all the while that you had selected a different suit or more impressive shoes that morning. As you begin to step into the room you trip in the doorframe and narrowly miss a dive-roll entrance! "Well at least I didn't pass out or throw up," …you think.

There's no time to wipe the rivulets of sweat from your palm or your brow before you're being introduced to the president of the company and his team of minions. The big handshake leaves you wondering how in heaven he could have missed how nervous you are. Never mind, he hasn't missed your nervousness – he's casually wiping his own palm on his Armani suit. You've lost this deal, and you haven't even opened your mouth to say anything of

93

substance yet. "Must be a dream!" You think. No.

True story. It happened to me. Okay, so maybe I embellished the team of minions. But I did lose the deal, and I am so glad that I did! This unsuccessful meeting prepared me for every other *successful* meeting I've had since.

Eleanor Roosevelt once said, "We gain strength, and courage, and confidence by each experience in which we really stop to look fear in the face... we must do that which we think we cannot."

Meeting with bank execs can be a bit scary and quite intimidating, so is writing this chapter!!! That is exactly why I'm here. I believe you need to do something that scares the heck out of you every day.

Let's rewind for a moment. I think we are all meant to walk down a certain path in life. We just need to stay vigilant, notice the signs and listen to our instincts. If I look back at my life, at every decision I've made (good or bad), at every door I've opened or closed, and every opportunity I've chosen to take or forgo – they have all led me to where I am today. It's almost serendipitous.

As a little girl, when all the other little girls were dressing up as Cinderella or some other imaginary princess, I was putting on mommy's heels and trench coat and grabbing her briefcase to play "businesswoman." I decided early on that I wanted to buy my own castle and not wait for the prince to buy it for me. Why am I sharing this story? Because you need to practice every day for the kind of life you want to lead. *Regardless of what your dream is, the road to success is paved with the same set of rules.*

I was fortunate growing up to have my mother as my first inspiration to succeed in business. My mother is a strong businesswoman who has always been my guide on how to conduct myself in the business world. If you don't have your own strong businesswoman mom, or aunt, or friend as your role model, allow me offer you a few of the tidbits of inspiration I have garnered during my journey to self-discovery.

TIDBIT #1 – HAVE A CLEAR VISION

Remember when you were a kid, someone asked you "what do you want to be when you grow up?" Among many others, a few of my answers were: teacher, event planner, aesthetician, make-up artist and spa owner. Although my answer to that question has changed several times since I was a kid, I realized that most of my answers had a common denominator. I want to be in charge of my own success (and I really wanted to have *CEO* on my business card).

Have a clear vision of your dream; of your business; of your life. Ask yourself why. "Why do I want to accomplish this? Why do I want to go this route?" Once you can answer why you wish to do something, the next step is HOW.

Personally, I like to work backwards. I decide *where* I want to be and *when* I want to be there, and then work backwards to today. For example, lets say your vision is to own a cupcake store in two years time. Where do you need to be in 18 months for you to achieve your goal in two years? Where do you need to be in 12 months to achieve your 18-month goal? Continue working backwards and assess the following things: What resources will you need? Who are the people you need to be involved on your team? What other steps do you need to take to get there?

Create a timeline of the steps you need to take --this breaks it down into manageable tasks. Keep some flexibility in that vision and tweak it down the road. Later you can come back to that vision to make sure it is still relevant and allow yourself to be able to measure your successes or failures along the way.

TIDBIT #2 – CHANGE PATHS,
IF YOU WANT/NEED TO

Whether you're looking for a job or working on a project for your business, many of us begin on a road that seemed like the right idea at the time. When I was in college, teaching seemed like a good field to be in. Half way through my program, I decided that I'm no longer interested in teaching and now I want to study aesthetics. During that program, I got a job with a tele-marketing company, which seemed to have potential advancement opportunities so I decided to change direction again. In the 3 years that followed I must have changed direction 7 or 8 times. Today I understand how important it was for me to have each experience, because they all play a part in the way I run my business today.

I know change is scary, but I also know that just because it worked yesterday, it doesn't mean it's going to work tomorrow. Don't get comfortable; comfort can lead to complacency. If it's not the right opportunity, know when to let it go. The biggest thing to remember is to not be afraid to stand up and change direction.

TIDBIT #3 – PUSH YOUR LIMITS

Sometimes, we strive so hard to look good in other people's eyes that we are afraid to step out of our own boxes. We are afraid to run that extra mile, take that next step, take on a new job position, or go to a boss/partner and put forth a business plan because we fear being judged; we fear failure but most of all, we fear success. Like everything else, success comes with consequences. When you succeed, people notice, they comment, they may even ask for advice. So instead, we set limits for ourselves, we procrastinate, and we don't take action.

Before you set limits for yourself, consider if there are unmanageable challenges that are holding you back or keeping you from your path? Or are they roadblocks that you created to keep yourself from the possibility of success? Have you considered the opportunities that you are giving up every day?

I am at a point in my life where I need to push my limits and work my buns off so that even if I fail, it will not be for lack of trying! If I succeed, as I have and plan to continue, it will be the reward of hard work. And I'd rather deal with the consequences of my success as opposed to the consequences of my fears.

TIDBIT #4 – REDISCOVER THE ART OF LISTENING

True listening is an art and it's fast becoming a lost one. Our lives move at such a fast pace and we are so consumed with our own needs, that sometimes we don't take the time to listen. Listen to our spouse, listen to our customers, or to our boss or business partner. If you take a moment during your next conversation, you may find that you are in one of two positions. You're either talking or you're getting ready to talk. There is a little voice in your head that starts assembling a response before it even gave you an opportunity to process the message it's receiving from the other side.

About four or five years into my business, a copy machine sales-man walked into my office. The timing could not have been more perfect. My company was growing and I needed to upgrade so I agreed to meet with him on the spot. As soon as he sat down I said, " this is your lucky day, I need a copier and you want to make a sale" He chuckled and pulled out a big thick booklet out of his briefcase. He then started telling me about the history of his company. I stopped him almost immediately and said, "look, I don't have much time and I already know what I need to know about the company. All I *want* to know is which machine is going to address my needs and how much it will cost me." His answer was, "I'll get to that, let me tell you a few things about the company". To which I responded, once again, "I don't care about the company history, I just *want* to know which machine you are going to sell me and how much it will cost me." To my amaze-ment and frustration, he was adamant about going through *his* process as oppose to listening to me, so I showed him the door. Two weeks later in walked another copy machine sales guy (from a different company). Reluctantly, I agreed to meet with him. He too pulled out his presentation binder and before he opened his mouth, I said, "Listen, I know you guys have a specific sales process, but I'm not interested in the history of your company. I'm interested to know which of your products fits my needs and what the cost is." Without saying a word, he put the booklet back into his briefcase, pulled out the pamphlet with the various products, made a few suggestions, gave me price / financing options, and 20 minutes later made a sale. I have been dealing with that company for almost nine years and have purchased several other machines from them.

When you listen, you understand people's true needs, wants and concerns. When you give people exactly what they need /want, you build trust, strengthen relationships, earn respect and, therefore, acquire loyalty.

TIDBIT #5 – PRINCIPLES + INTEGRITY = SUCCESS

I live my life by three simple principles: I want to shake people's hands and look them in the eyes, I want to go to sleep at night with a clear conscience, and I never want to have to look over your shoulder. You can go from being really big to a "nobody" overnight. Things can change in the blink of an eye. My credo has always been that to maintain longevity you must always be authentic, honest and ethical. If you are in a job or on a path that doesn't allow you to be true; get off it. My litmus test is this: if I lost everything today, would my reputation and relationships survive the fall?

Be what you say. Be authentic. If you went to dine at a beautiful, 5-star restaurant you would think by the décor that the owner takes pride in his establishment. How would it change your perception if you found out that areas like the kitchen, that you could not see, were filthy or infested? Be mindful of the areas in your life that people cannot see. *Integrity is doing the right thing when no one is watching*.

There are so many inspirational tidbits I have gathered over the years; it would take several books to share them all.

So I leave you with this great quote from Benjamin Button: **"For what its worth it's never to late… to be whoever you want to be. There is no time limit, start whenever you want. You can change or stay the same… there are no rules to this thing. You** can make the best or worst of it. I hope you make the best of it… and I hope you see things that startle you - and I hope you feel things you never felt before – I hope you meet people with a different point of view – I hope you live a life you are proud of – if you find you're not, I hope you find the strength to start all over again. "

About Orit

Orit Koren co-founded First Class Financial Services in 1998. Ms. Koren has earned an industry wide reputation for her dedication to professionalism and keen eye for business opportunities. First Class Financial Services provides financing and leasing services to several hundred independent Used Car facilities across the Province of Ontario, Canada. Her company enjoys its success, and partnership with lenders across Canada, due to her drive and due diligence. It has been her mission to bring unparalleled administrative services and fraud prevention processes to her industry.

To learn more about Orit Koren or First Class Financial Services Inc., visit: www.fcloans.ca or call 1.866.30LOANS

CHAPTER 10

"You become what you believe. You are where you are today in your life based on everything you have believed." ~ Oprah Winfrey

The Online Expert: How the Internet Can Build Your Brand, Grow Your Business and Inspire Success

By Lindsay Dicks

It's a website that draws more than seventy million page views and over six million users a month. It also generates 20,000 emails every single week from visitors.

And it's all due to the power of one woman.

I'm talking about Oprah.com, the official site for anything and everything Oprah Winfrey has her hands on. That includes her magazine, her TV shows, her cable network, and Oprah radio. For women who mean business, Oprah is the absolute gold standard. Her brand extends to every major form of media available.

However, there's only *one* venue where all of her massive media power converges – the only place that has the ability to showcase everything she has to offer in both a convenient and impactful presentation – and that's her website. If you want to let the world know you mean business, the Internet is the place to do it. When you utilize the many online tools available to brand yourself as the celebrity expert in your field, you'll find it's not only very affordable, but also the easiest way to reach your past, present and potential customers. It's also the most effective way to communicate what you want to communicate about your brand and your business.

THE BASICS OF BRANDING

I've seen time and time again that successful branding really begins with one core principle – "People buy people." We may admire the way corporations and companies operate – but we don't invite them out to dinner or send them Christmas cards. We're human beings and we relate best to other human beings. That's why, at our Celebrity Branding Agency, we focus on *who* our clients are first – and then on what they do.

This is a lesson that all the greats understand. Just like Oprah, business superstars like Donald Trump and Richard Branson continually build their companies' visibility by making themselves as prominent as possible – they write books, star in TV shows, make guest appearances on other TV shows whenever they can and stamp their personalities right on top of each of their endeavors. Before they could do that, however, they had to introduce and promote who they were to the public.

A perfect example of that is someone I love both for her cooking *and* her branding - Rachael Ray, who accidentally discovered the power of personality for herself. She began her career by teaching a class on her famous 30-minute dinners as well as demonstrating the meals on the local news, when viewers asked her to put all the recipes in one place. She assembled her first cookbook, got it published and it was an immediate success.

But the book wasn't what made her brand "pop" – that happened as a result of a last-minute invitation to appear on "The Today Show" during one of the worst snowstorms the Northeast had ever seen. With her mother's help, Rachel made the 150 mile car trip to the New York City studios, where all of America got their first good look at Ray and her winning personality. The appearance was the true first step to the Rachael Ray phenomenon.

People like Rachel Ray, Oprah and other female business entrepreneurs like Martha Stewart built their personal brands first - and their business empires second. They started by growing a fervent fan base, and the books, magazines, and TV shows grew from that base - not to mention the multi-million dollar corporations.

When you make yourself the story, people get interested in who you are and what you're doing. You develop fans and followers that admire your expertise and want more from you. That means you grow your audience, you continually uncover new leads and you constantly create a new flow of customers for your products and/or services.

And that's what it's all about, right?

MAKING THE MOVE ONLINE

Your online presence begins with your website. Like any other personality-driven site, it has to sell you and your expertise. That means including plenty of content and creating a dynamic site that's always evolving, instead of a static "brochure" site that no one ever bothers to visit more than once. This means making a certain investment in your website that will continue to pay you plenty of dividends over time.

Here are a few features a good branding website should make sure to focus on:

• **Promoting Your Personality**

There's a reason almost all of the homepages of our clients' websites feature large photos of them, and, in some cases, an introductory video. This isn't because we are narcissistic; in fact many of my clients fight me on it – until they see that it works! What we want is to make sure that visitors instantly get a sense of who they are. By putting a face to the name, we immediately make a personal connection. A video (like the one you'll find of me on our CelebritySites.com home page) that welcomes you to the site is even better at establishing that personal connection.

• Demonstrating Your Expertise

Testimonials, credentials, endorsements, published works, accomplishments - whatever you have that displays your knowledge and experience in your field of business should be prominently featured on your site. Third party verification - what other people say about you - always goes a long way towards establishing your credibility.

The other important way to demonstrate your expertise is by providing valuable content. Blogs, articles, and videos giving helpful hints or giving more in-depth explanations of your products and services help the visitor see that you know what you're doing; it also provides added value to your site. The more you can update this content the better, as it will ensure that your "fans" will return to your site on a consistent basis to see what's new.

• Defining Your Benefit

Here's another big customer question that every business person – male or female – needs to be able to answer: "What's in it for me?" In other words, how does what you do help the average person coming to your site? Benefit-oriented headlines and copy help potential customers see exactly how *your* expert abilities will provide *them* with a measurable advantage. For example, if you're a personal trainer, you can tell your visitors that you can help them lose 10 pounds in 30 days (or whatever your program's results are). The more specific you are about the results, the more those results will resonate! Remember, it should speak to THEM!

• **Raising Your Ranking**

Your website should be specially designed to hit a high note when it comes to Google search rankings. If your site doesn't rank high, you have a problem. A big percentage of traffic to any business website results from search engines such as Google - and if your website doesn't show up on the first page of those results, you're losing potential visitors and income. There are many special techniques that can be employed to make your site an SEO (Search Engine Optimization) superstar - for example, videos add a lot of extra impact as far as Google is concerned - and we make sure that every one of our sites takes full advantage of them.

• **Spotlighting Your Social Media**

Social media, which we'll discuss in a little more detail soon, is all-important to spreading your message and burnishing your brand. It's also the best way for your fan base to stay in touch with you on a regular basis. That's why Facebook, Twitter, LinkedIn and other social media services should be strongly integrated into your website design. You want to make it easy for visitors to "follow," "like," "subscribe" and "connect" to you through every virtual channel possible. Social media updates are also a great way to keep your website current – by programming your home page to feature your latest tweets, blogs and postings, you add new content without doing a lot of extra work.

• **Powering Your Profile**

Your site should look as professional and polished as possible, both in its design and in how it presents you - so that it will appeal to members of the media. When reporters and writers are looking for a reputable quote or a business to feature in a story, they look for someone credible who is an expert in their field to help. And you – yes, *you*! – can be that person. Many of our websites have attracted media attention to our clients. If you've already had national or local magazine articles or media stories done about you, make sure they're prominently featured so the media can see you've already proven yourself in their arena.

• Growing Your Fan Base

One of the most important attributes of any successful business website is the ability to generate leads and collect contact information. If a visitor comes and goes without leaving a name and an email address, that's leaving potential money on the table. At the same time, you don't want to hard-sell someone into buying something at that very minute.

That's why a great tactic is to offer free information in exchange for contact information – it could be a special report having to do with your field of expertise, a webinar that informs as well as sells your product or service, or any other kind of content. When you offer your visitors something of value, they are more willing to give you their email address.

This is also an excellent way to build up your "fan base," as we like to call it. As many marketing gurus will tell you, your database is your "hidden goldmine" – having the contact information of people who have already demonstrated an interest in what you do means you have the perfect group to build a relationship with – putting you in an ideal position to ultimately gain their business.

BRANCHING OUT WITH YOUR BRAND

Your website can be compared to an old-fashioned brick-and-mortar store, in that the store can't go to its customers; its customers have to physically go to the store. On the Internet, it's the same thing – people have to go to your site, which is both good and bad. The good is that your website showcases you the way you want to be showcased – you control the design, the look, and the content. It's completely designed to sell you and your business, just as a store would be.

The bad? In the case of both the store and the website, you have to find ways to drive people to come to them. Otherwise, they're like that tree falling in the forest – it might make a sound when it hits, but it doesn't matter if nobody's there to hear it.

A store doesn't make money unless people know it's there. So storeowners have to get the word out through a variety of methods – direct mail, ads in the paper, sponsorship of community events and so forth. Your website (and your brand!) is no different. No one is going to pay attention unless you go to where *they* are and tell them where *you* are.

That's why the rise of social media over the last few years is so important to branding yourself as a celebrity expert online. Social media is the ultimate tool to promote your brand and your website - and not only that, it's (for the most part) absolutely free to use.

Think about Facebook for a moment. Did you know, if the total population of that site formed a country, it would be the third largest country in the world? With more than 800 million users worldwide, can you imagine a better place to promote your brand?

Then there's Twitter. Facebook may beat it in sheer numbers, but Twitter is awesome at putting out quick updates and links to new content on your website. Not only that, but there are many free software platforms that allow you to update Facebook and

Twitter statuses simultaneously, saving you some work.

And don't discount LinkedIn. The world's biggest professional social media site is heading towards 150 million users. As of September 30, 2011, the site was adding new members at the rate of two *every second*. There are also many specialized professional groups on LinkedIn that you can easily join, network with and also add to your credentials page.

Finally, there's the new player in town, Google+, which was launched in the summer of 2011. With a membership of over 60 million in that short amount of time, it's definitely worth watching to see how this site develops.

How do you best leverage these sites? Well, start by keeping your fan base apprised of whatever you're doing that reinforces your celebrity expert status. Maybe you've written a book, or will be speaking at a seminar – let people know. When you add new content to your website, "tweet" about it and provide a link to drive traffic over. If you're profiled in an article, interviewed on a show, or having any other "media moment," make sure you let everyone know all about it.

And, at the very least, continue to demonstrate your expertise by offering short, valuable tips whenever you can. If people are deriving a benefit just from your social media statuses, they will learn to trust you and they will pay more attention to your business offerings. They will also spread the word about you and gain you even *more* fans.

There are many other methods to build your online celebrity brand – through online press releases that can be strategically placed, for example, as well as with YouTube videos and partnerships with other online businesses that complement yours.

As long as you are offering consistent value through your online marketing efforts, you should be like a snowball rolling downhill – picking up more and more leads and growing bigger and bigger along the way.

Anyway, that's the way we "roll" at CelebritySites.com and CelebrityBrandingAgency.com – where I invite you to stop by to find out more about how online celebrity branding can make you a cyber-superstar!

About Lindsay

Lindsay Dicks helps her clients tell their stories in the online world. Being brought up around a family of marketers, but a product of Generation Y, Lindsay naturally gravitated to the new world of online marketing. Lindsay began freelance writing in 2000 and soon after launched her own PR firm that thrived by offering an in-your-face "Guaranteed PR" that was one of the first of its type in the nation.

Lindsay's new media career is centered on her philosophy that "people buy people." Her goal is to help her clients build a relationship with their prospects and customers. Once that relationship is built and they learn to trust them as the expert in their field, then they will do business with them. Lindsay also built a patent-pending process that utilizes social media marketing, content marketing and search engine optimization to create online "buzz" for her clients that helps them to convey their business and personal story. Lindsay's clientele span the entire business map and range from doctors and small business owners to Inc 500 CEOs.

Lindsay is a graduate of the University of Florida. She is the CEO of Celebrity-Sites™, an online marketing company specializing in social media and online personal branding. Lindsay is also a multi-best-selling author including the best-selling book "Power Principles for Success" which she co-authored with Brian Tracy. She was also selected as one of America's PremierExperts™ and has been quoted in Newsweek, the Wall Street Journal, USA Today, Inc Magazine as well as featured on NBC, ABC, and CBS television affiliates speaking on social media, search engine optimization and making more money online. Lindsay was also recently brought on FOX 35 News as their Online Marketing Expert.

Lindsay, a national speaker, has shared the stage with some of the top speakers in the world such as Brian Tracy, Lee Milteer, Ron LeGrand, Arielle Ford, David Bullock, Brian Horn, Peter Shankman and many others. Lindsay was also a Producer on the Emmy-nominated film Jacob's Turn.

You can connect with Lindsay at:
Lindsay@CelebritySites.com
www.twitter.com/LindsayMDicks
www.facebook.com/LindsayDicks

CHAPTER 11

Secrets to Setting Yourself Up For Success As a Woman Entrepreneur

By Rachel Cosgrove -
Co-Owner of Results Fitness

Being a woman in a male-dominated industry, the fitness industry, I am used to attending conferences and being one of a few women in the room, used to working among more men than women, and finding my way to be taken seriously and climb the ladder while staying feminine. You might be thinking…but the fitness industry has plenty of women? The majority of women in my industry take the route of aerobic/spinning instructor, yoga instructor, pilates instructor or other mind/body "softer" avenues within the fitness industry. I was drawn in the direction of strength and conditioning, spending the majority of my career teaching people how to lift weights properly – along with athletic conditioning and what seems to be considered more masculine – attracting more men than women. Although, part of my mission is to change that, because I believe being feminine and strong complement each other and bring out the best in every female I have worked with. I currently manage a team of mostly male trainers at my gym that I co-own with my husband.

What this chapter is NOT:

- This chapter is NOT a man-bashing, "we don't need them" chapter. Men and Women need each other. In industries, like the fitness industry, women bring something completely different to the table, complementing what men offer. Working together, men and women can bring out the best in each other. Figure out a way to contribute something different and complement those around you, instead of competing.

- This is also NOT a "Woe is me…I'm a female…" chapter. If you think you should get a break because you're a woman, forget it. One of the companies I work for has 80 different speakers – all speaking on some aspect of fitness to other personal trainers. Of the 80 speakers, 4 of us are women. Every year the host gets request for more women speakers. The problem is – there aren't any women applying to speak who are qualified and able to hold their own against everyone else in the line up. I don't have a spot presenting because I am a woman, I have a spot as a presenter because I can hold my own in the line up with all of the other talented speakers who happen to be men. End any "poor me, I'm a woman" thoughts and instead figure out how you can become the best at what you do and offer something that complements the others who are successful in your industry.

This chapter IS about reaching your potential, becoming the best at who you are and what you do, so that you can offer more to whatever industry you are in. Now let's get down to business…

WHAT DO YOU WANT?

You are going somewhere within walking distance and ask me for directions. I tell you turn by turn how to get there. "First, you will walk out of this door, turn left and go down the stairs, cross the street… " When you left my office you looked down at your feet and watched each footstep you took as you followed my directions. I watched as you ran into a wall because you took a little too hard of a left turn, you missed the stairs the first time and you didn't really know where you were or if you were on track to get to where you wanted to go – because you wouldn't pick your head up to see. You looked at each footstep one after the other without picking your head up.

Pick your head up! You have to look up and see exactly where you are going while you are on your journey to get somewhere. Most women are focused on the day-by- day "To Do" list. Figure out exactly where you want to go, and everyday pick your head up and make sure you are getting closer to where you want to go.

As women we are very good at being busy. We know how to multi task, we know how to take on a million responsibilities. But we are not good at deciding what it is we want, exactly what we want and making sure every action we take is getting us closer to what we want.

We don't want to be selfish. Usually, in the role of caretaker our days are spent making sure everyone else is taken care of; it is hard to let go of that and decide, "What do I want?" …feeling guilty that if we go after what we want we are being selfish.

Remember this: You are not helping anyone by keeping yourself small and not going after what you are meant to do, have and be.

Action Step: Take 5 minutes to write down your stream of conscious thinking (without putting too much thought into it, and instead let your subconscious do the talking), in a few sentences exactly what you want. What is your ideal day? What opportunities are you taking advantage of? How much money are you making? Create a goal board or vision board that you will see everyday to "pick your head up" and see everyday, keeping you focused on moving forward toward your goals and vision for your business and life.

LEARN TO SAY "NO"

Once you know exactly where you are going, it is time to learn to say "No." Any opportunity, responsibility or anything that will use your time, ask yourself – will this get me closer to my goal? If yes, then next question is – Can I delegate it? Do less better, and you'll have things fall into place to accomplish your goals much faster.

Action Step: Say No to something today and see how great it feels to not take on every responsibility that comes your way. This will allow you to get laser focus toward what you want and are meant to accomplish.

BE CONFIDENT

Lack of confidence is one of the number one reasons women hold themselves back – ...afraid to put themselves out there, ... afraid they aren't good enough. As long as you know more than the audience or client you are standing in front of, you have so much to offer!

We each have our own journey where we have learned our own lessons. Every single one of us has experiences and knowledge that we can help others with. You have come to some conclusions in your life after the experiences you have had – why would you keep those conclusions from anyone else?

Action: Get in front of an audience that you are confident in front of and start to groom your confidence that you do know what you are talking about. When that voice of doubt creeps in, replace it by planting a positive seed. This first audience might be a school, speaking to a group of kids. Start to share what you know with others, and gain the confidence you need to be the best you can be, and offer others everything you have to offer.

TAKE CARE OF YOU

The #1 most important responsibility you have is to take care of yourself. You may not realize it, but your family, your employees, your friends and your colleagues are all looking to you to lead them. If you are stressed out, they will all be stressed out. If you aren't taking care of yourself, they will think it is ok to stop taking care of themselves. Taking care of you is more important than anything else on your "To Do" list. Be a leader and make yourself your #1 priority.

Action: Make yourself a priority on your schedule. Plan to exercise, pack your food to eat healthy, book a massage, take some downtime. I highly recommend using strength training as part of your exercise routine for all of the benefits it has – including the mental boost it gives you – feeling stronger and able to take on anything that comes your way!

Rachel Cosgrove co-owns Results Fitness: (www.results-fitness.com) and has her own website at: www.rachelcosgrove.com.

About Rachel

Rachel co-owns and operates Results Fitness with her husband Alwyn Cosgrove, a fitness center in Southern California for over 11 years. It was voted one of the top 10 gyms in the United States three years in a row by *Men's Health* Magazine. She earned her Bachelor of Science in Physiology at the University of California at Santa Barbara and holds her CSCS with the National Strength and Conditioning Association. She has also been certified by the International Society of Sports Nutrition, USA Weightlifting and with Precision Nutrition.

Rachel has been featured in numerous magazines including *Muscle and Fitness Hers, Men's Fitness, Men's Health, Women's Health, Oxygen, More Magazine, Runner's World, Women's World, Real Simple, More Magazine, Shape magazine among others.*

She currently has her own column in *Women's Health Magazine* and is the best selling author of the book *The Female Body Breakthrough,* published by Rodale in November 2009. She has also been interviewed on television on Fox, ABC and WGN numerous times discussing her book and sharing her message.

As one of the featured speakers for the company, Perform Better, she lectures nationally and internationally on topics such as strength training, fat loss, business in the fitness industry and nutrition specifically for women, helping them to reach their potential in all aspects of their life.

Rachel is also an athlete herself. She is an Ironman Triathlete and has been to the World Championships on Team USA for triathlon. She has also competed in Power Lifting and Fitness competitions. Extremely goal-oriented, she is always looking for a new physical challenge and draws from that experience – making her a better coach.

As a spokesperson for Secret Deodorant and Nike, she has also been a consultant for Gatorade, Nike, *Women's Health and Men's Health* Magazines.

She and her team at Results Fitness strive to become the best part of their member's day, achieving results and changing lives while having fun doing it! They are on a mission to change the way fitness is done.

You can learn more about Rachel at: www.rachelcosgrove.com and Results Fitness at: www.results-fitness.com.

CHAPTER 12

THE SAVVY CHICK'S GUIDE TO NEW MEDIA

Why It Doesn't Pay To Be Anti-Social

By Laura E. Kelly

Every time I meet with a new client of **Savvy Chick Media**, we discuss the goals they have for growing their business. It has become increasingly difficult for companies, especially in this economy, to cut through the clutter to advertise and market their business. In these meetings, I am always asked the following questions:

"So how does **Savvy Chick Media** plan on advertising and marketing my company?

TV, yellow pages, radio, or billboards?

And should we start using these social media sites I hear so much about?"

If you own a business, you probably have the same questions. Before I share with you the **Savvy Chick's** Guide to New Media, let me address the traditional ways of advertising/marketing and then explain why you should discard the old and embrace the new.

WHAT IS THE DIFFERENCE BETWEEN ADVERTISING & MARKETING?

It does not matter what kind of business you have built. If you do not have clients, if you do not have some mechanism for bringing in new business, your business will die. Period.

(A) **What is advertising**?

"A **paid public** promotion for some product or service."

There are two very important elements to that definition.

(1) **paid**:It costs money!

(2) **public**: It is viewed by the masses. Though the goal of the ad is to reach a specific target, your ad will still be viewed by more than your target audience. It is a non-personal presentation.

(B) **What is marketing**?

"The planning and implementation of a strategy to promote one's product or services to a targeted audience."

It is more of a process designed to identify a business's potential client base. Once the target is specified, methods and systems are utilized to continually communicate with that potential customer. It is not intended to reach the general public. Because it is targeted, it typically costs much less than traditional advertising.

Marketing is the "relationship" that you develop with potential clients and clients. Advertising alone does not guarantee you will attract new business. It takes more. Advertising alone does not guarantee you will keep that client once they hire you. It takes more. Advertising alone does not guarantee you will have that client as a "repeat" client or a referral base, regardless of how "good" you were for him/her. Advertising may make you and your company well known, but notoriety does not matter if you are not signing up and keeping your clients.

And exactly what are you marketing? You are marketing yourself. People are buying you. Most people fail to realize this principle. Advertising may work great with products. You can get away with selling some product like a toilet bowl cleaner with traditional advertising. You don't need that great attachment or "relationship" with that product's "scrubbing bubbles."

But advertising alone will not work in the long run - you need more.

The old maxim is forever true. If a client loves you and your services, he/she will tell two or three others about you and your business. If they hate you, they will tell twenty people. Successful marketing will bring you in contact with a lot of people. The way in which you respond to them and their needs will influence how they speak of you and your business. To increase the power of your "relationship marketing", you must increase the size of your marketing umbrella. You must increase the reach, the effectiveness, and the frequency of your contacts with people with whom you already have a relationship.

There are a variety of ways your business can _advertise_ using the OLD, TRADITIONAL MEDIA:

- Television
- Yellow Pages
- Radio
- Billboards

I shall give you the **Savvy Chick** thoughts on the pros and cons of each.

(1) **Television**

One of my clients, Gary Martin Hays, a very successful personal injury attorney in Atlanta, is a big advocate of television advertising. One of the first questions I asked him was, "How do you effectively advertise using television?" His response, "Spend, spend, spend. In the Atlanta market, you will be competing against law firms that spend over $200,000.00 per month just on television commercials. These firms have not just popped up overnight. Most of the big spenders on TV in the Atlanta market have been around for over 10 years. To cut through this clutter, you must spend equal to or greater dollars to get noticed with a very creative ad strategy."

Pros:

- TV is a quick way to get your message out to a lot of people
- You control frequency, placement, and budget
- You can track calls with a special phone number for each ad
- This is not a fixed cost as you can pull your ads for a week or longer, if necessary

Cons:

- Expensive
- Very expensive
- Unbelievably expensive
- Very difficult to compete with necessary frequency
- Must be willing to keep or increase your budget for a minimum of 24 months
- It is a "Shotgun" approach
- Cable TV and satellite TV are cutting down viewership on major channels.
- The Analytic Consulting Group released a report written by E. Craig Stacey, Ph.D., that concluded "long-term advertising is at least twice as effective as short-term advertising and payout should be calculated over at least a two-year period."

Death of the 30-second spot: Another thing to consider is the declining TV audience on network television due to channel fragmentation. For example: In 1998, an estimated 76 million people watched the final episode of *Seinfeld*. This accounted for 58% of in-use televisions according to Nielsen Media Research. This sounds like a lot of viewers until you compare it with the number of viewers that watched the final episode of *MASH*. In 1983, there were an estimated 105 million viewers (a 77% share). And in 2004, the final episode of *Friends* only had 51 million viewers (a 43% share).

In summary, TV is not what it used to be.

(2) **Yellow Pages**:

One big thing to remember about advertising in telephone directories - If someone is looking through the yellow page ads, they are there because they have a specific **_need_**. They are not browsing. They are trying to fill a need. This type of advertising is often referred to as "needs" based. People go to the directory because they need someone to help them.

Pros:

- If they are looking in the Yellow Pages, they are a HOT prospect
- You can control the creative content
- You can track calls with a distinct phone number
- The fact that you have an ad in the directory gives you some credibilitywith potential clients.

Cons:

- Fixed cost; you can't spend more or less while the current book is out
- There are a LOT of ads in the book
- Very inflexible - If your business changes, you can't

change the ad until the next book comes out

- There are a LOT of phone directories out. Not only do you have competition within the book, you have competition amongst the different books

(3) **Radio**: Everyone assumes that radio is a great way to reach potential clients, especially if you are in a city that has a long commute. But there are several problems with this assumption.

 a. Today, people are tuning out commercials. There is no more station loyalty. As soon as the songs are over or the radio personality finishes, the listener either turns the station or mentally turns off the radio until the songs return. It has truly become short attention span theater.

 b. Radio is expensive!

 c. Listeners often do not try to write down a company name or number while driving.

  - XM and Sirius are making huge in-roads on a daily basis.

  - Cars now have the MP3 or I-Pod plug in options where you can play your personal library of music or self-help audio tracks instead of listening to the radio.

There are only few instances where radio has worked for my non-profit client, Keep Georgia Safe.org:

- When the founder and the executive director appeared on radio shows around the city, it gave them instant credibility with the listening audience.

- It also helped when there were specific fund-raising events the charity could promote.

How can this work for you?

- If you can get a well-known, well-respected radio personality in your area to endorse you, then his/her listeners will also give you their seal of approval.

But remember this **Savvy Chick** rule:
If you plan on using radio, you must do it often. Frequency is the key during morning and afternoon drive. Ads at night and on weekends are just clutter.

(4) **Billboards**:

I do not like billboard advertising. Period. These are expensive. It is very difficult to track the results. You may have a lot of "views", but how many of those are turning into calls? If you are going to use billboards, you must use them in conjunction with a big media blitz for "branding" purposes. For example: you are new to the market and you are trying to get the name of your company out there - if you have the money, then use TV, radio, and billboards. But with billboards, not only do you have the cost of renting the board, you must pay for the production of the wrap used. Will someone sitting at home that needs your business or services remember your billboard - and more importantly - your phone number?

Back to my new client meeting and discussion:

My clients and I are quickly in agreement that the OLD, TRADITIONAL MEDIA is not working well in today's economy. So we get to their next question:

"**Savvy Chick** - How can I Advertise and Market my business using NEW MEDIA?"

Let's talk about *New Media* for a moment. Social media has crept its way into our everyday lives and it has now become a very useful marketing and public relations tool. In the last five years, there has been an incredible shift in the way people learn, buy and communicate. Internet speeds are faster than ever and social media audiences are rapidly expanding. By the end of 2011, there were over 800 million active Facebook users. The average Facebook user has approximately 130 friends and is connected to 80 different pages or groups. Over 200 million were added in 2011 and the numbers are steadily increasing.

WHAT'S SO "NEW" ABOUT NEW MEDIA?

Relationships. New media encourages interaction with customers, creative content generation, instant feedback and the use of new technologies. At **Savvy Chick Media**, we embrace and use the following New Media tools every day for our clients:

(i). Facebook

(ii). Twitter

(iii). NEW Search Engine Optimized Websites through WebSocial.ly

Let me explain each one, and discuss why you should be using these tools as well.

Facebook

Facebook is a social networking site that connects people to friends, family and businesses. For business purposes, **Savvy Chick Media** updates client pages daily with creative posts, photos, videos, contests and campaigns. The goal is to have an interactive page that is constantly updated and providing our "Friends" with helpful information and interesting content. We are always looking for innovative ways to increase the reach of our "Likes" and "Friends" so we can continually engage and market with them. If you are not incorporating Facebook into your marketing mix, you are behind the times. Chances are - your competitors are already using it.

But please remember this important **Savvy Chick** rule:

"DO NOT have a Facebook page for your business if you don't know how to use it properly!"

You will be doing more harm than good!

Here are a few **Savvy Chick** Tips for Facebook business pages:

1. Post plenty of photos. For the restaurant, I like to post pictures of the daily specials or new dishes. Fans respond well to visuals and they like to see what you are doing.

2. Ask questions. Asking a question sparks conversation with your fans and gets them involved. Ask their opinion of a product or service you provide and respond to their feedback.

3. Post every day, but only once a day. Don't over crowd your fans with messages. Keep them short, sweet and to the point. If you post too often, they may "unlike" your page.

Twitter

Twitter is essentially a mini-blog mixed with instant message. It allows you to post quick, concise updates with a limited number of characters. It's a great tool to keep customers informed about what is going on without spending a long time writing up a blog post. **Savvy Chick Media** uses Twitter on a daily basis to keep customers in the loop with short witty updates.

1. Add links. Because twitter limits your message length, add a link to take your followers to a blog post or a photo.

2. Be original. Personalize your profile and your tweets. Don't be afraid to say what you think, but be professional!

3. Be active. Retweet information posted by others that could benefit your business and respond to other people's tweets. Find a hash-tag and join in on the conversation. This will give you more exposure in return.

WebSocial.ly

And last but not least, what makes **Savvy Chick Media** so "savvy" is a website company called WebSocial.ly (www.websocially.com). WebSocial.ly has created a socially optimized website platform using WordPress managed hosting that allows me to post from the website to the Blog, Facebook and Twitter all in one click. It also allows to me create email blasts from my blog posts to send to my customer databases. I haven't found any other website solution that comes close to the Websocial.ly platform. It is so user-friendly.

Savvy Chick has proven through all of her clients that traditional marketing is too expensive and ineffective to compete in today's economy. Remember it always pays to BE social! For helpful hints on how to use the new media to promote your business, check out: www.savvychickmedia.com.

About Laura

Laura E. Kelly is the owner and operator of Savvy Chick Media. She lives and works in Atlanta, Georgia. Laura graduated from Georgia Southern University with a degree in Journalism. Her professional background started with public relations, working with restaurants, small businesses and non-profit organizations. She quickly moved to specializing in new media. Some of her key clients include:

Keep Georgia Safe – www.KeepGeorgiaSafe.org
www.facebook.com/keepgeorgiasafe
www.twitter.com/keepgeorgiasafe

The Law Offices of Gary Martin Hays & Associates
www.GaryMartinHays.com; www.facebook.com/TheSafetyLawyer
www.facebook.com/GaryMartinHaysLaw
www.twitter.com/GaryMartinHays

Gary's Bistro – www.GarysBistro.com
www.facebook.com/GarysBistro
www.twitter.com/GarysBistro

She also provides articles and updates for the Elizabeth Smart Foundation (www.ElizabethSmartFoundation.org). When Laura is not working for her clients at Savvy Chick Media, you can find her food blogging on www.ViciouslyDelicious.com, running marathons and dishing up culinary creations in her kitchen.

CHAPTER 13

Boardroom to the Bedroom:
7 Fail-Proof Secrets to Save Your Business AND Your Marriage

By Susan Jane Kirkpatrick

Going into business with your spouse requires tremendous commitment to each other, shared values and goals, and the ability to maintain a comfortable sense of balance between work and your personal lives. To be sure, being a Couple working together in an Entrepreneur Business or as I like to call being a **"Copreneur Business,"** is an exciting adventure that will enrich your lives in many ways.

But a Copreneur Business can also be a quagmire of pitfalls and potholes – a potentially discouraging and disheartening experience because being Copreneurs "raises the stakes" in your relationship – by bringing prosperity, career satisfaction and personal growth to those who succeed, but frustration, financial struggle, animosity and heartbreak for those less fortunate. I have experienced both.

THE SHORT STORY

At the end of my college days, I set off to find a J-O-B and that journey led me to New Mexico. I started to date my future husband, a veterinarian, who also moonlighted in real estate (a family tradition).

He convinced me to go to real estate broker school at night. I didn't really want to go. Heck, I knew nothing of selling. I used to make my father buy all my Girl Scout cookies so I wouldn't have to go door-to-door.

My future husband and I formed a little real estate company, even though I knew absolutely NOTHING about running a business (or being successful at a business!) particularly a real estate business. I was scared, I had no background on being an entrepreneur and I did not have a strong sense of self. I certainly didn't believe I had any abilities to bring to the business table at the ripe age of 22. Because of my lack of self-esteem, I realize that a lot of my years were lived based on someone else's advice about what was best for me.

We did not discuss our vision; we had no sense of mission in our venture – not even a business plan (I never heard of such a thing). Here was the plan he laid out: He does the selling; I do everything else when and how he says so.

We were not married or even yet engaged, when my future parents-in-law gave us the chance to run their family ranch. What a great opportunity! I never thought a **"Jersey Girl"** would ever get to live on a real working ranch! I took the leap of faith and moved to a tiny little town deep in the majestic Rocky Mountains.

I cooked, cleaned, fed kids and ranch hands, bucked hay, sheered and castrated sheep, worked as a veterinarian assistant, and learned how to ride, gather cattle, and fix fences, hunt, fish and pretty much do all a ranch gal should know how to do. I did all the bookkeeping for the ranch, the vet clinic, our tiny real estate business and the hunting and fishing business. After 3 years, we were married in 1983.

We never gave a second thought about what our respective roles were in our ranching and real estate businesses, or even what our marriage relationship was all about. We never discussed our vision beyond "make more money so he could travel and not work." We never shared our life goals and we did not distinguish what mattered most in our lives – mine, his, or ours. We still didn't have a business plan! We got caught up in the "busyness" of "newness." I never felt comfortable airing my fears.

I began to see warning flags; little "red lights" that I didn't heed – arguments over attitudes, over responsibilities, over respect. **Money was always an issue.**

When we argued it always boiled down to the point that I had a good "job." I was afraid to *"rock the boat."* My fear was if I disagreed I would be thrown out, penniless, a bag lady. We had fights where I was told I could go with my mattress and my cat; exactly what he said I brought into the partnership and the marriage. I hated these fights. I avoided them at all costs. I didn't have the tools to deal with the conflict or the ability to help my husband understand me. My early ignorance on things like self-awareness and personal growth tools or success strategies set up a ticking time bomb deep within me that sputtered all through our relationship.

Luckily I had a wonderful mother-in-law. She asked me to join her little real estate office in town. I managed the day-to-day operation of the office and I enjoyed it. I liked making things tick, serving customers, clients, staff and the sales agents. I continued to "do the books" for the ranch, the real estate office, the veterinarian business, the hunting and guiding business and also for our NEW tree farm business and our logging enterprises around the valley. PLUS the responsibility for all the house work, cooking and shopping, organizing home maintenance projects, not to mention planning and managing our social life, vacations, and business travel arrangements – it all fell on my plate.

In 1990, I owned the real estate company outright. I hired a personal assistant. Our customer and clients became savvier so I decided to make the little real estate business into a World Class Business. I even came to understand the true concepts of selling. I had a knack for listening to client's dreams and desires and being able to pick their perfect properties for them.

But the growth of the real estate business put wear and tear on my marriage:

- We argued all the time over my new broker manager.
- My spouse's style of hostile competition wreaked havoc on my relationships with the agents to the point where agents quit.
- He was jealous of the time I spent working on the real estate business.
- No matter how hard I tried to keep our fights out of the office, he liked to fight in front of people, especially my staff. I had a tough time diffusing these situations and most of the time I failed.

Yet, despite all the problems, our businesses really began to take off. I learned effective Business Strategies that enabled me to leap frog competition and accelerate the success of the real estate business.

But on the inside, I just couldn't handle it all anymore; it was getting to be too much. Important items started to fall through the cracks. I didn't know how to say NO. And I couldn't keep anyone happy, least of all myself. I tried to run another half marathon and I broke down with stress. And my marriage was in serious trouble. I was convinced that everyone and everything depended upon and relied upon ME.

I was feeling frustrated, confused, fearful, lonely, trapped and overwhelmed.

Finally, the time bomb exploded and my marriage did not survive. I believe that looking at others to blame instead of at ourselves was at the root of our disruptive relationship.

Looking back on this experience, I believe if we were not so distracted and distraught with the marriage relationship those businesses would be even more successful today. With the clarity of 20/20 hindsight, I see that:

- The dysfunctions of the marriage were magnified in the businesses.
- Our marital issues horribly affected the business decisions we made.
- My ex-husband and I could not communicate in a way that each of us could actually hear and understand the other.
- My choices were dictated more by fear instead of my values.

I vowed to change. I learned many lessons from my previous Copreneur Businesses. I figured out over the years what worked and didn't work in developing a really successful business. And I even still believed that the "husband and wife" business team was the way I wanted to live my life.

I launched my own personal in-depth study and research project on many successful and not-so-successful Husband and Wife Business Teams. I was looking for answers. I wanted to know the WHY behind my mistakes, so I would know HOW never to make them again.

Although there are many reasons businesses and marriages fail, I found seven 'secrets' that are universal to the couples I researched.

1. THE SECRET FORMULA "US FACTOR™"

MC + BV + PG = Us

Marriage Commitment + Business Vision + Personal Growth = "Us Factor"

My research shows that in a committed marriage, *the feeling that their partners are helping them to advance their relationships, their careers, and realize their ideal achievements* is an important issue. The meaning you make of your relationship together is the _most significant factor_ in determining the success of your business and marriage. Ask yourself and your spouse this question, "What is your *perception* of how supportive your spouse is to you (and vice versa)?

2. BUSINESS VISION: YOURS, MINE OR OURS

Not every couple is meant to be in business together and not every couple has what it takes to be a successful Copreneur Team. One of the most important steps to take in determining if you "got what it takes" is to do an assessment of your Visions, Goals, and Priorities as they fit into your overall Life Plan and share that plan with your spouse. Add this to your "US Factor" equation above.

3. DON'T GET LOST IN THE TRANSLATION

Don't make assumptions about what you think your spouse knows, how they will react to things, or even what their interpretation of a situation might be. Instead, ask questions and try to gain clarity. *Similarly, be careful in choosing words; say exactly what you mean so that there can be no misunderstanding of what you are saying.* Always be thoroughly honest, and don't leave out important details.

You may want to enlist the support of a third party, such as an independent advisor, business coach, or other professional. Do not feel that you must sacrifice your own value system or integrity in order to avoid difficult conversations. This is the very problem I faced in my previous marriage. I just couldn't muster the courage to have that difficult conversation with my husband. And living so far from anyone to lend a safe haven for a conversation only made the situation more frightening for me.

4. PATROL YOUR BORDERS

Boundaries are an agreed set of rules to live by that encompasses everything you do, both in the workplace and elsewhere. Boundaries, of course, go well beyond physical space; the times and circumstances under which business issues may or may not be addressed should be considered. Many couples, for example, agree not to discuss business on Sundays. The important thing here is to clearly delineate between when business issues can be raised, and what is reserved for your personal life, and agree to respect the boundaries between them.

5. R.E.S.P.E.C.T.

Having a working relationship with your spouse has its special problems. Your marriage becomes a relationship with higher stakes than that of other couples who are not Copreneurs – there is more at risk for both of you.

You are at the crossroads of both a love relationship and a business enterprise, where your personal and financial issues intersect; to be sure, both your relationship and your wealth can be "in the balance" when you are Copreneurs. *Are you treating your spouse like a business partner or your business partner like a spouse?"*

The point that I am making is that there are forms of conduct that may be appropriate for one context, but not the other. But in any case, you owe it to your spouse and yourself to show respect wherever you are and whatever you are doing.

6. DIVA OR HEROINE? DEFINE YOUR ROLE

In order to succeed at working with your spouse as a business partner, it is necessary for the two of you to agree on what roles you will play in the business. This should be done in sufficient detail so that there are no ambiguities about your respective responsibilities. As you go about this process, consider what your individual strengths and weaknesses are. What do you like to do, and what are you good at doing?

Be honest about your commitment to the business as well; is

your business something that you really want to immerse your-self in, or is it more of your spouse's business, with you playing a lesser role?

Delegating tasks back and forth, and being accountable to each other, is part of the process of working together. Remember, you are creating a system of mutual dependency that, due to your special relationship, goes way beyond ordinary teamwork.

7. BALLROOM DANCING

Working together as business partners, and living a life as husband and wife, requires that many things work together effectively, and all at the same time. It's like ballroom dancing, where you learn the subtle – and not so subtle – nuances of working with your partner. You need to learn their style and anticipate how they move, and interact with you when you are together. It demands a heightened sense of awareness and a meshing of styles, like the components of a complex dance routine all fitting together and working smoothly to achieve a common purpose.

This is your "Us Factor" in Motion!

About Susan

Susan Jane Kirkpatrick is the co-founder (along with her husband Steven) of AdvantaCoach, an executive & small business coaching, consulting, training, and education company. AdvantaCoach is a distinctive blend of their unique entrepreneurial experience and professional knowledge from each of their respective fields of expertise. Their programs are easy and simple systems specifically developed for Entrepreneurs and Copreneurs to successfully develop and profitably grow their businesses. With new clarity and focus, motivation, and inspiration, Susan and Steven know that when Entrepreneurs regain their original passion for their business and lifestyle they quickly grow their business and achieve greater success.

Susan has over 30 years experience as a New Mexico Real Estate Broker and small business owner and Copreneur. Susan is the former Owner/CEO of Northern New Mexico Real Estate, Inc. a franchisee of the United Country Real Estate Franchise. Her real estate office was consistently in the Top Ten performers throughout the nation for 5 years. Shortly after joining the United Country organization, Northern New Mexico Real Estate, Inc. achieved the #1 Office position within the entire United Country National Franchise System (out of 650 offices nationwide) with more than $23 million in sales revenue. This was accomplished in a small town of only 800 year round residents, and where the nearest traffic light is 81 miles away! Also, Susan was the Business Operations Manager of her family ranch and was instrumental in its successful land development and sales.

Susan holds a Bachelor of Sciences degree in Secondary Education/ English from Glassboro State University (now Rowan University), New Jersey. She is a Certified Professional Coach with the Coach Training Alliance (CCTA) and Fowler-Wainwright International. She is a certified administrator for the Meyers-Briggs Type Indicator (MBTI) Step I & Step II.

Susan is an avid sportsman, scuba diver, lover of history and good food. She has travelled the world doing her favorite things: dove shooting in Argentina, Peacock Bass fishing in the Amazon, scuba diving in Indonesia, indulging in delicious food in Italy, successfully navigating the Tokyo Metro system (!), and many exciting photo safaris in South Africa. Happily transplanted to Virginia (along with her dog and six cats), she lives her dream with her husband Steven. She is thoroughly enjoying her new home in Hampton Roads by spending her free time gardening, hiking and swimming, and she is planning the purchase of her new boat!

CHAPTER 14

Strategic Partnerships: What You Need When You Have Nothing

By Tammy Levent

PART 1: MY STORY

I had owned our jewelry store with my then-husband in Florida for five years when robbers stole ninety-percent of the inventory, forcing us to close. Six months later, my grandmother passed out at the wheel of her car and crashed into the brick wall of a house while driving my two young children, ages nine and two. My grandmother died in the crash, my son and daughter woke up in the ICU with severe injuries. The life we had been building was lost in less than six months. House payments and medical bills piled up; our savings quickly drained.

Sometimes fate can hit you so hard all you can do is reel from the blow. I didn't know how to start living my life again, how to get my identity back, how to even begin to rebuild. But at some point, you have to stand up – for your family and for yourself – and take hold of your inner power to survive. I believe women have infinite power in themselves to create the lives they want, no matter what their challenges are, no matter what circumstances made up their pasts. How do you begin to build the life you want? Strategic partnerships are what you need when you have nothing.

I was sitting in the ICU, having just quit a telemarketing job I took after the jewelry store went under, consumed with uncertainties. I didn't know if my daughter would be able to speak again or if my son would lose his eyesight, and I didn't know how I was going to keep our home and care for them. I was so worried over the circumstances limiting me that I couldn't see how to move forward. While I was chatting with one of the nurses at the ICU, she asked me, "If it had nothing to do with money, what would you do?" That simple question made me start thinking of what I *could* do instead of what I couldn't do. I replied with the first thought that came to mind: "I would travel the world."

I had a goal again, but no background in the travel industry, and I still had to pay our bills. For my entire professional life I had been in sales – I co-founded my first company at the age of 17 – and I could sell anything to anyone. I took the closest job I could find to the travel industry: telemarketing cruises to nowhere. "Congratulations, you've won a trip to the Bahamas!" (For four days you'll be bombarded with timeshare sellers on a boat in the Caribbean). I apologize.

I was quickly promoted into training new telemarketers – "Tammy the Trainer," they called me – but I still needed to make the leap into working at a legitimate travel business. Once again I felt trapped in my circumstances and I lost touch with my sense of having control over my life. At the last holiday party, my trainees had given me a gag gift of a small whip, and as I sat at my desk drilling telemarketing wisdom into new recruits over the phone, I started playing with it. I'd practice aiming and whipping a single pen out of my pen holder.

Whipping around office supplies requires focus, and more than a little coordination. It's a small, silly thing, but when you feel like you have no control over the big things, finding that you have control over something small is significant. It's easy to feel like your circumstances define you, but the truth I found – through whipping pens out of cups – is that we have infinite power to control our futures. Incredible Women Have Infinite Power In Themselves. I WHIP IT is now the inspiration for my web series, *WHIP IT OUT SHOW with Tammy Levent,* and my professional "WHIPshops™" workshop series for businesswomen. Men can join in as well, if they dare.

Beginning with Strategic Partnerships

Through an ad in the paper, I applied for work at a legitimate travel agency doing corporate sales. At this point, I had years of experience selling, and each time I landed another big corporate account, I'd tell my boss "look at all this business I'm bringing in, you need to give me more money." I have never been shy. Even though I was bringing in accounts from companies whose names you'll find on every aisle of the grocery store, my boss stood like a barrier to expanding the business. He was happy with things as they were, but after two years, I felt I had to pursue my ambition.

I called my rolodex of corporate travel clients, told them I was starting my own company, and asked them to follow me. They said they would follow me wherever I went. My problem was that even though I had clients, I had nowhere to go. I didn't have enough money for my own office, much less money to hire employees to answer phones.

I sat at my desk, wondering how I was going to get out of this job, and opened up the Tampa Bay Business Journal. By fate or chance I found exactly what I needed: A feature article listing the top travel agencies of Tampa Bay. The agencies listed first were franchises, too corporate to allow me to do what I planned. I scanned down the list until I found an independent travel agency listed at number seven. I called the owner and said, "I'll give you thirty-percent of my profits for a desk, phone line, and a fax machine." With this arrangement, I could start my company under my own brand, Elite Travel, with no overhead; he got thirty-percent of profits from my base of corporate clients by giving what cost him nothing – he loved the idea.

Try it. Call someone and tell them you want to give them thirty-percent of whatever you make in return for something that costs them little or no money. Who would say no to that? That is a strategic partnership.

Building a Business with Strategic Partnerships

After a few years, I sensed changes in the travel industry. Corporate travel was slowing down with the economy, and suddenly companies viewed expensive trips for executives as liabilities instead of perks. I left my corporate travel partnership to pursue a part of the travel industry that remained unaffected by the economic downturn: destination weddings and honeymoons. The problem was that even though I had a strong background in corporate travel, I had no experience planning other types of vacations.

At a business seminar, I won a trip to a Sandals resort by sheer chance. Since I was running my own business, I couldn't find time to take the trip myself, but I had an idea. I asked the resort if I could use the trip as an Elite Travel giveaway at a bridal show. Again, it wouldn't cost the resort anything, and it wouldn't cost me anything out of pocket, but both of us would benefit from attracting brides to our companies through a giveaway. The strategy worked so well that Sandals' competitor, Couples resorts, noticed and offered me 187 trips to give the next year.

Once I had trips to use for promotions, I partnered with the bridal show producer, becoming a sponsor of the shows through donating trips, which meant I didn't even have to pay for my booths at the shows. In addition, the show producer promoted my brand and our giveaway, along with including my company in full page advertising in their magazine, which has nationwide distribution.

These initial partnerships brought my company from making two million dollars gross income to making multi-millions. And, to this day, it costs me nothing. Fifteen years later, I'm still working with the same people, helping to build their brands as we all work together to build mine.

Building a Community with Strategic Partnerships

Three years ago it occurred to me that while I was becoming both a national and global brand, I was ignoring the business that could be found in my own hometown. In the last few years corporate travel has hit an all-time low, and the economy has forced many couples to postpone their honeymoons, and even their weddings. Once again I needed to find another source of income. I needed a strategic partner who would get me in touch with people who still had money to travel.

Ruth Eckerd Hall is the top small performing arts center in the world with a reach of 180,000 people who see their advertisements in print, online, and at shows. It's located only a few miles away from my office, and their season ticket holders have the discretionary income for luxury travel. I called and offered to donate two-percent of the gross sales I made from clients referred to me through Ruth Eckerd Hall to the performing art center's charity. Using my other strategic partnerships, I also gave them trips they could auction off as prizes at their fundraisers. In return, my name and logo are on their social media, billboards, posters, flyers, and programs. We've already booked thousands of dollars of travel together.

The same strategy that worked for me with honeymoon resorts and bridal shows is now working for me with Ruth Eckerd Hall's audience and luxury resorts. Luxury resort vendors are strategically partnering with me to reach a new audience they couldn't otherwise access – their brands appear at events and on every social media update, billboard, flyer and program too, giving them free advertising and brand recognition.

However, bringing in charities has an added benefit: When you involve charities, your community will rally behind you to help build your brand and invest themselves in your success. Turn your business mindset into giving instead of getting, and you'll be amazed at how much more you get out of it.

I believe that you should never disregard anyone, because you never know when they'll be exactly the person you need. But what I believe even more is the power of women, the power I have myself, not to be defined by our pasts or the circumstances that would limit us. Today, with credit markets drying up and banks gripping every dollar with white-knuckled fists, it's easy to think you can't start or expand your business. Even when you think you have nothing, I guarantee you already have what you need to start living the life you want. Remember, **W**omen **H**ave **I**nfinite **P**ower **I**n **T**hemselves. *Whip it,* ladies.

PART 2: FOUR STEPS TO BUILDING YOUR BUSINESS WITH STRATEGIC PARTNERSHIPS

Put down your business plan and start thinking in terms of where you want to be, what you have to offer, and who can help you reach your goals.

1. Where do you want to be in five or ten years? Make a list of friends, vendors, business owners and organizations that can help you get there. Chances are, you already have people in your life who are ready to help, and whom you can help in turn. If not, don't be afraid to cold call and sell your plan.

   Example: To reach your long-term goals, you need to form partnerships that will grow and last. The only way they can do that is when benefits are equal for everyone involved. I worked with *Perfect Wedding Guide*, one of the largest wedding publications in the U.S. for years, because they got as much out of the trip giveaways I offered as I and my resort partners got from their free ad space and bridal show presence. Through this partnership, we grew our brands together.

2. What do you need from your strategic partner to achieve your next goal?

Example: To successfully launch my new I WHIP IT motivational speaking series and web show, I needed media exposure in a big way. I contacted S.E. Day, host of the *Legally Steal Show*, and asked him to partner with me in a separate series of workshops, called "Got Money?" that would make the most of both our areas of expertise – business strategy for me, money strategy for him. His brand is already on radio and television, and I WHIP IT has an online show, podcast, and is backed by the local Business Journal. By joining to grow our brands together, we have all our combined media working to reach a wider audience of businessmen and women.

3. Now ask yourself: What can your partner get from you?

Example: I was looking for a fun location to host my WHIPshop™ series and found an ideal VIP lounge at a performing arts center. I approached the president of their nonprofit foundation and offered to bring her twenty new patrons – the twenty women attending my workshop who had probably never seen the place before. I suggested she give them a tour of the newly renovated facility, which gave her the opportunity to show off the property to potential investors. And of course, I got a free location!

4. Tie it into a charity, either a pre-existing charity or one you've created to help your community. When you build your community along with your business, everyone will want to help spread the word, and your brand.

Example: My birthday party doubles as an annual charity event to raise money for Friends of Joshua House, a safe-haven for abused, neglected and abandoned children. By partnering with other local businesses, I pay almost nothing for an off-the-hook party where other business owners mingle and form new strategic partnerships. While drinking "Tammy-tinis," we make thousands of dollars for one of my favorite charities.

As you bring all your resources together to form strategic partnerships, you're building your brand, making money, and helping your community. That is a powerful combination that will survive any changes that the economy, or fate, can throw at you. Maybe *you* will be my next strategic partner.

About Tammy

Tammy Levent: Entrepreneur, Travel Expert, Author and Renowned Speaker

Tammy Levent devotes herself to helping other women discover the power they have to change their lives, no matter what their circumstances. She sums up her mantra of success in the acronym "I WHIP IT" – meaning Incredible Women Have Infinite Power In Themselves. I WHIP IT was born when Tammy held her first whip while sitting at her desk training telemarketers. For the first time in years, she felt like she had control. She took that feeling and ran with it.

With her new web series WHIP IT OUT SHOW with Tammy Levent at www.WhipItOutShow.com and her day-long WHIPshops™ that "take the work out of it," Tammy guides other women – whip in hand – to find their courage, declare their goals, and use strategic partnerships to make those goals happen. Unlike many speakers, Tammy doesn't stop at motivation; she gives immediately usable step-by-step instruction on how to create a business and lifestyle around your passion.

As founder and CEO of Elite Travel, Tammy has guided her company into the exclusive group of American Express Travel Agencies and garnered numerous awards. Elite Travel has been named a Platinum Preferred Agency Couples Resort for twelve years in a row; an American Express Vacations Global Award Worldwide Best of the Best Agency fourteen years in a row; and was "Ranked 3rd" in the Fastest 50 growing companies in Tampa Bay area in 2005, and kept the Fastest 50 status into 2006 and 2007. While Tammy plans hundreds of destination weddings and honeymoons every year, a highlight came in 2008 when she managed the celebrity "I do Redo" wedding for NBC's Biggest Loser couple, Amy and Marty Wolff, on the island of St. Lucia which was featured on Extra! Tammy's travel expertise has appeared in publications around the country including Perfect Wedding Guide, Brides Magazine, Modern Bride, The Robb Report, and Condé Nast Traveler®.

Single mother of Katie, 26, and Jordan, 20, Tammy Levent lives in Tampa, Florida with her better half, Rob. She owns an impressive collection of whips.

For more information on Elite Travel, the WHIP IT OUT Show, and WHIP-shops™, visit TammyLevent.com.

Tammy Levent
Tammy@TammyLevent.com
www.Whipitoutshow.com
www.elitetravelgroup.net
www.TammyLevent.com
Tel: 1-866-726-9090

CHAPTER 15

How Do You Measure Success?

By Rene McGill

Ask several people that question and most will put a dollar sign in front of their answer. Others will give you a picture of the lifestyle they want like – where they'll live, how they'll spend their time, who they'll spend it with, what they'll buy, and so on.

It doesn't matter what your definition of success is, have you defined the work you need to do to get there? Are you measuring the results along the way so you know if you're on track? How are you spending your time? Are you getting the return on your investment that you expect?

These seem like simple straightforward questions that anyone can answer. But have you ever been so busy switching gears in your business or at your job, you question if you're even heading in the right direction?

I think most of us have, at one time or another. With technology changing at warp speed, and the amount of information we're processing, we're often so busy reacting to things it's easy to lose sight of your goals and plans. You can look up and realize that weeks or months – maybe even years – have passed since you really sat down and took stock of where you're at in the big picture.

As an "entrepreneur-by-default" who has turned into a "serial entrepreneur," (I married one!) will be quick to admit that I'm often so busy "doing" things (I have owned and operated multiple businesses), I don't have time to stop and think Sure, we think about the project at hand, but do we actually stop and think: Is "THIS" project or chore actually going to get me closer to my goals?

When I joined my husband Jerry in business full-time, he felt like he was dragging me kicking and screaming into what would become our business today. I didn't have a business degree in management, finance and accounting and all the things I thought you should know BEFORE you went into business for yourself. With a degree in journalism and a minor in English, I was a newspaper reporter and had expected to spend my professional life writing in one form or another. Sure, I spent a couple of years just after we got married doing clerical jobs in the corporate world to help pay the bills by day and lay the groundwork for our business by night. But I thought I'd do this for a few years and go back to my profession.

Even after a couple of years part-time, I still didn't feel ready to make the jump to a full-time entrepreneur. And I had just been offered a technical writing job that I was ready to accept.

But – at the same time – things were really picking up steam in what was soon to become our current business, Liquid Assets, a beverage wholesale business that specializes in blending and manufacturing cocktail mixes for restaurants and bars.

Jerry and I knew it wouldn't be long before we needed more help to run the company. I just wasn't sure I was that person. Later I would learn that having "skin in the game" (meaning a vested interest) meant I was probably the best person for the job.

So on a Wednesday night after work, Jerry and I drove an hour and half to meet with his dad. As a stockbroker, financial planner and entrepreneur himself, he could see exactly where we were headed. The three of us agreed it was the right time for me to make the jump. So, the very day I planned to accept a new corporate job and get back to writing, I went in and gave my two weeks notice.

I would soon discover one secret to the entrepreneurial world — you don't have to know how to do everything going in. You just need to know where to go for the right help, how to implement it and how to monitor the results. It's like piecing together a jigsaw puzzle.

Even after 14 years of our company growing and evolving, I'm still learning and putting pieces of the puzzle together. Sometimes I've felt running a business is like a giant puzzle. You have all these pieces you need to fit together to see the big picture. And if you've ever put together a puzzle, you know how helpful it is to have the box with picture on it to show you the way.

Would it help if there was a "box" that shows the big picture of your business as you piece it together and helps you monitor the results along the way?

Well like that box, I found an illustration recently that literally shows the things we've been doing the past 14 years. In the confines of this chapter, I can't tell you everything that has worked and everything that hasn't. But what I can do is share this "big picture" or "the box" with you, so maybe you can put yours together faster and easier.

Years ago when we began studying direct response marketing through Glazer Kennedy Insider's Circle, Dan Kennedy and Bill Glazer would drill into us the phrase "if you can measure it, you can improve it."

This is a very powerful phrase that is not limited to just your marketing. When you measure things – whether formally gathering data and comparing it or simply noticing trends and patterns – you are arming yourself with information. Use this information and you can leverage your success.

Recently, our company Liquid Assets was chosen to participate in Goldman Sachs 10,000 Small Businesses, a nationwide program of practical management training and information to spur growth in the small business sector. With Warren Buffet on the advisory board, Goldman Sachs underwriting the program and Babson College (a leading institution for entrepreneurial studies) developing the curriculum, I fully expected intense study on finance and growth strategies. It was no surprise that one of the first modules we studied was "Money & Metrics." Of course we focused on interpreting traditional financial statements – Balance Sheets, Income Statements and Statements of Cash Flow.

But we also spent time defining other measurements – or metrics – in our businesses and how to use them. I was even surprised by one of the tools they call a Business Dashboard.

Like the "dashboard" on your car, it provides systematic diagnosis everytime you start the engine. You check the same items at the same time so you can see any changes.

The business dashboard is a grid that gives you a visual layout – or snapshot – of the "metrics" in your business. It has the three sections with the top half of each section devoted to "metrics" that currently exist in your business and the team you have in place. What are your goals? How much capital do you have to work with? What's your plan? Who do you know? It's what you have.

The bottom half of each section takes it to the next level by identifying and adding items you need to improve your business. What are the tactics you'll use to achieve those goals? What are the metrics you'll use to measure your progress? Who else do you need to know? It's what you need to run at peak performance.

A surprising part of the dashboard for me was the first section called "You." It's actually the first section you see. The dashboard gives "You" equal – and visible – space, right beside your business needs so you can measure success as a whole.

Whether you're an entrepreneur or a stay-at-home mom, you've probably got dozens of stories of how often you've overlooked yourself – hopes, dreams, leisure time or even your health – in a relentless pursuit of taking care of business. Unless you make New Year's resolutions or use a time management program like FranklinCovey, you can get bogged down with busy work and sometimes crisis management and neglect yourself.

Although some people have a formal list of personal goals, others just have some hopes and dreams rattling around in their head. Whichever one describes you, you'll be a lot more likely to fulfill them if you have them written down right beside your business goals and plans.

Short-term, there will always be situations when it makes sense to delay or skip something personal. It's just going to happen. Maybe you have to skip a friend's barbeque because you have an important deadline. Maybe you have to put off that trip to Europe because of a bad economy. You just don't want to miss every barbeque. If Europe's your dream, don't miss it because it never got on your calendar or planned for in your budget.

Like the adage we use about people – "the squeaky wheel gets the oil" – your time and money can get sucked up by lots of "squeaky" things in business and in life. Make sure "YOU" get the attention you deserve. Write down your personal goals beside your business goals, decide what you need to achieve them, and "measure" your progress consistently. If you've gotten off track, you'll realize it and can adjust.

After all, if you continually neglect your personal list, you're probably defeating the very reason you want to be successful in the first place. Once again ... "if you can measure it, you can improve it."

Now, moving on to the business section where the obvious measurements are your financials – the Statement of Cash Flows, Income Statement and Balance Sheet. These are the things you're probably – *hopefully* – measuring consistently. You probably compare them to a previous time period so you'll know if your financial health is improving, declining or staying about the same.

On your financials, you may find it useful to compare them to not only your performance in previous periods, but also to other similar businesses. Here's a resource you can check out: It's a publication called the Annual Statement Studies® produced by the Risk Management Association (www.rmahq.org). It's a comparison of data that comes directly from financials of small and medium-size business customers of institutions that are members of RMA.

This is one tool accountants, consultants and bankers can use to compare your financial position and performance to other similar businesses. In this annual guide, you can look up businesses similar to yours and compare stats like annual operating expenses, total assets, and long-term debt. It also has a section on the ratios professionals use to monitor business stability. If you don't have a finance or accounting background, you may need to have your accountant or a competent business advisor help you analyze and interpret these figures. But it can give you a good rule of thumb to see how you stack up to the competition.

There are even computer programs that do similar comparisons for you. We used one called ProfitCents. It takes your financial data and converts it into reports you can use to compare to other businesses in your industry. Your accountant should be able to plug your data into this program or refer you to someone who can. (We used ProfitCents through the Small Business Development Council in Houston.)

So what's the Small Business Development Center (SBDC)? It's another resource. SBDCs are partnerships between the government and colleges/universities administered by the Small Business Administration. Their objective is to provide educational services to small business owners and entrepreneurs. Google SBDC to learn more and find the one closest to you.

They're a wealth of information, and since it's funded by tax dollars, you've already paid for the services. Use them! In addition to their free help and resources, they also sponsor classes and workshops by local experts. The fees are nominal and you can trust the instructor has been screened for competency. That's a real time savings.

If you own a business or operate any part of one, you're probably measuring other things all the time; sometimes consciously, sometimes unconsciously. By measuring something, you're gathering useful information, which will tell you if you need to make adjustments.

So what are some other "metrics" to watch in your business? How about the ones talked about or tracked by your industry. Besides revenue and profit, you can probably rattle off a number of different "metrics" that your industry monitors. They're common formulas or ratios that people in your line of work understand and use. They're everyday tools used to make changes that affect revenue and profit.

These metrics are easy to spot when you pick up an industry publication or online newsletter or read the descriptions of seminars at a trade show or conference. If it's an important measurement in your industry, it will likely get attention in these places.

Let's take a look at some of these:
- Restaurant owners and managers watch food costs and how many times they "flip a table"
- Own or operate a bar, then it's pour cost or cost per ounce to watch closely
- A manager of an automotive repair shop probably knows how many cars he repairs in an average month
- A distributor/wholesaler knows how many times they turnover inventory

This is nothing new to most of us. When you're ultimately responsible for an operation you figure out really fast what things affect you. You're probably measuring things or looking at the "metrics" without even realizing it.

One of the metrics Dan Kennedy exposed us to in marketing is the lifetime value of a customer. Wikipedia defines the term like this: "the net present value of the cash flows attributed to the relationship with a customer. The use of customer lifetime value as a marketing metric tends to place greater emphasis on customer service and long-term customer satisfaction, rather than on maximizing short-term sales…"

It's a long definition, but very helpful to change your focus from short-term to long-term so you don't get hung up on immediate expenses. It gives you an objective way to decide how to invest your dollars to get and keep customers. The key word is value. Again, Google "lifetime value of a customer" and you'll access a lot of information.

Hopefully you've thought of a few metrics aside from your standard financials that can make a difference in your business and you can develop your own "dashboard" to monitor them consistently. Whether it's daily, weekly, monthly or quarterly, it's a safe bet you'll get the big picture faster and be able to leverage your success faster than operating without them.

If you want to steal a few ideas that other business owners have shared? Or hear how one gutsy business owner ignored her industry norms and why? I've posted more examples of metrics and how you can use them on my website: www.renemcgill.com. Best of luck to you!

About Rene

Rene McGill is co-founder of Liquid Assets, a family owned and operated beverage wholesaler based in Houston, Texas, that has catered to the restaurant and bar industry for the last 14 years.

Rene received her degree in Journalism from Texas A&M University in 1988 and was a newspaper reporter covering local government and education. When she married and moved to Houston, she worked for Hines Interests while she assisted her husband Jerry in starting their own business in the beverage wholesale industry.

Rene left Hines in the mid 1990's and went to work for Service Corporation International in Trust Administration. In 1996, she left SCI to join Jerry full-time in running the family businesses.

During her time running Liquid Assets, she added to an extensive writing background with several years of study in direct response marketing under the direction of Dan Kennedy. Rene and Jerry have used these direct response skills to change and grow their existing businesses as well as consult with a variety of business owners on techniques to market their businesses. She and Jerry started and ran the Glazer-Kennedy Insider Circle chapter in Houston for three years before selling it to focus on their existing businesses. Together they have also started and operated three additional businesses besides Liquid Assets.

When time permits, Rene does copywriting and editing for other direct response marketing projects and is active in the Greater Houston Restaurant Association.

CHAPTER 16

I AIN'T NO SLOUCH
Tales of Posture in Business

By Dr. Amelia Case

There is something regal - even magical - about a woman who stands up straight, looks people in the face and simply breathes normally. Maybe the impression starts with the storybook characters who always have perfect posture. Say what you will about Cinderella or Sleeping Beauty or Little Red Riding Hood. There is one thing we all find irresistible in them: they share the unusual appearance of being upright. No slouching for these ladies. But this isn't a story about fairytales. It's better than that. It's a story about who you are when you are Certain; when your body language reveals you've put your stake in the ground and claimed your land, your earth, your space, your territory, your path.

It's impossible to be certain, feel certain or act with certainty while you are slumped into a round-shouldered ball. Honey, if you are Certain, it shows. It doesn't only show in your sparkling eyes, easy breath and settled shoulders, it shows all over. When you are Certain, the tension in your body is balanced, revealing a tone that unites its various parts. Poise just takes over all of your cells, and your bearing reveals what's present: Light. Like a sundial at noon, you cast no shadow.

SHOULDERS BACK. SHOULDERS FORWARD

There was a time when I wanted to be in my own business so I could tell everyone what to do (and, perhaps, to go to hell). I wanted to feel the power; to tell people how to do things Right. I had a sharp and critical mind, knew what I wanted, and was bursting with the details of my ideals. The staff were my pawns, necessary for the execution of my imaginings. My expectations of their performance were low, but that was no surprise. They didn't have the good fortune to know what I knew, so it was my burden to have to tell them. So, tell them I did. It was my way or the highway. I'll admit it wasn't much of a credo, but it worked - for a while. Until it didn't.

I found out micromanaging people or telling them to go to hell isn't management, isn't leadership - and isn't good for business. It was hard to keep employees, hard to get people to rally for any purpose, and hard to communicate (particularly because my willingness to listen didn't really exist). I had some great experiences observing how the power of my emotions affected others, but the bigger outcome didn't feel satisfying. Micromanaging or telling people to go to hell isn't a great way to build a team or keep a customer. And, to make things worse, constantly checking up on my staff was boring and took up too much of my time, robbing me of my vitality. Throwing a fit when they were in error (no matter how clever my words were or how quickly I could reduce my opponent to surrender) left me narcoleptic. So, over time, my fantasy (of not needing anyone - or anyone else's opinion) faded away. As I let that persona go, my body started to look - and feel - different. It began to soften. The shoulder girdle that had been held back in a ready-to-fight stance, with all the tension amassed in my upper arms, ready to throw a punch – breath held in - started to change. My spine (that had been stuck in an overzealous arch) came up to a healthier balance, and I released my breath. Thinking back, I realize that fighter-posture wasn't upright, it was *self-righteous*.

After the failure of my first attempt at leadership (ruling by force, intimidation and temper), I tried something else. Like a pendulum ruled by the laws of physics, I swung the other way, surrendering myself to the intelligence of my staff, patients and anyone else who had a good idea. They were full of potential, and I had finally recognized the missing ingredient: Others! I had learned my lesson! My heretofore resentment of other people turned to infatuation with what they could make possible. Support was the name of this game. I wanted them to put their fabulous ideas into effect. I didn't want to tell anyone to go to hell. I wanted to tell them how much they all meant to me and the business; how much I needed them, and how important they were to our success. Of course, I never actually qualified their business acumen, accounting skills, or marketing prowess, nor did I want to burden them - or myself - with such pressures. I didn't want to criticize them with something called Quality Control. Oh, No! That sounded a bit too much like The Old Me. I had learned my lesson: No More Mrs. Meanguy: Overcritical and Micromanaging. Oh, did I listen! Oh, was I responsive! I had so many meetings. I smiled a lot. I fancied myself as a Servant Leader, ready to make everyone who worked for me happy. I'll admit it wasn't much of a credo, but it worked - for a while. Until it didn't.

I found out giving people unqualified support isn't management, isn't leadership - and isn't good for business. It was hard to keep employees, hard to get people to rally for any purpose, and hard to communicate (particularly because my willingness to give feedback didn't really exist). I had some great experiences observing how the power of my emotions affected others, but the bigger outcome didn't feel satisfying. Giving everyone the right to do it his way isn't a great way to build a team or keep a customer. And, to make things worse, coddling my staff and making them comfortable strained my resources and made me miserable. Enthusiastically supporting my staff whether they deserved it or not (no matter how much I surprised myself by my ability to be patient and tolerant) left me confounded and exhausted. So, over time, my fantasy (of supporting and relying on everyone, and listening to all their opinions) faded away. As I let that persona go, my body started to look - and feel - different. It perked up. After a prolonged period of looking like my chest was falling in, muscles slack - breath shallow at the end of a sigh - I started to come back up to see the horizon. The shoulder girdle that fell forward with disappointed weight, devoid of shape, started to rise. My spine, burdened with servitude, came back to a healthier balance, and I took in a breath. Thinking back, I realize that posture wasn't just humble. It was *self-wrongteous*. I'd gone too far, again.

CHAPTER 542: THE BODY'S HINTS

After the first 541 failures at trying to achieve my own Leadership Style (supported by umpteen books, videos and seminars), I surrendered. I didn't need another book or another lesson. I had plenty of great advice. What I didn't have was a reference point. Then, it hit me. I needed to pay careful attention to someone else really important: Me! Before I executed my day (and at the end of my day), I turned my attention to a finely-tuned instrument I already owned called my body. If something didn't feel right – or if I started to feel my body change its posture or function – I stopped to find out what was happening. If my shoulders were held too far back, and I felt an exaggerated fearlessness that thrust my spine into more of an excited funky chicken posture; if I found myself unable to catch up with my own breath, I sought to discover why I felt untouchable and invincible. If my shoulders fell forward and I felt an exaggerated hopelessness that weakened my spine into a limp noodle; if my breath was too easy to sigh into an exhale, I sought to discover why I was disparaging myself, or why I felt beaten. I realized my body was processing my life's adventure, and when I became conscious of that reliable feedback (in the form of posture and breath), I was able to alter my state – in a way that felt authentic and applicable to my world right then. I learned to fine tune myself; to find poise. *I* became my primary tool to identify my own Certainty.

My life didn't become easy or comfortable. I was regularly challenged and stretched out of my comfort zone. But, I stopped feeling so insecure, and scared. I started to have more answers than questions. When I honored the information my body gave me, it was easier to act, choose, and behave with more integrity. I felt certain on some higher plain of my consciousness even if I was an Inexperienced Beginner. Paying attention to the tension in my body, its posture, and how I was breathing was my elementary education in taking myself to a new level of personal power. I developed the self-confidence of an American Indian scout on the prairie, one who owned the environment by listening to the sound of the wind or feeling the vibration of hoofbeats on the plains. It was fun. More than that, it was working. I felt a balance of many forces coming together to create someone I could stand behind: Me!

It's my business to observe and respond to how the body functions. Yet, for a long time, one of the more simple and profound measures of my own wellness was overlooked. It was as if I was ignoring a great advisor or confidante. What was I thinking? I know this! The body never lies. It's worth paying attention to what it's saying. Everyday, if we are willing to look and to feel simple things, like our posture and breath giving us real physiological and anatomical truth about how we're tuned – about our own power - we get critical information to help us in our lives. Anyone who desires to have an edge – meaning an advantage in life – can appreciate this fact. What a bonus: Not only do we have access to highly valuable information about ourselves, we can even have it about others. Besides the fact that we are all mammals who have billions of years of instinct built in to assess non-verbal signals in other mammals, we are human beings who have the ability to observe and understand other human beings' emotions.

If you see someone sitting down with collapsed shoulders and a concave chest, you are not likely to perceive her as powerful. You might think she is sad, or maybe she needs to sit on the toilet. In the animal kingdom, there's a reason someone might target her for lunch. If you see someone standing up with her chest held high, chin up and shoulders back, you might think she is either a joking hysteric or maybe she has to burp. In the animal kingdom, there's a reason another beast would perceive a reason to attack. Both postures seem extreme, and off-balance. Just *not Right*. Imagine being that person. I can. I have been her. But remember, this isn't about posture. It's about how our bodies offer us information about ourselves, and how, when we pay attention to that information, we have the opportunity to evolve. It's about how we do get an edge when we use the finely-tuned instrument we were born with: Ourselves. After all, that's where we gave birth to the creation of our ambitions. Why not check in to see how the process sits within the place it was conceived?

The journey of being Certain as a woman who means business – who consciously intends to bring something valuable to her marketplace - is nothing if not a study in how to honor the unique self in the world. Through the gift of the trials and tribulations of trying on different personalities we all have the opportunity to find ourselves. And, in doing so, we find there's a little bit of a dictator and a little bit of a servant in everything we do along the way. When they are balanced, we are balanced. That's when we stand upright. When we are balanced, our projects, whether they are the companies or the families we build, reflect – as an extension of ourselves – that balance. Not only do we experience equanimity in our minds, but in our breath, bodies and creations. Every day is an exploration, a journey, a new experience; something that affects our bodies and minds. If we ignore ourselves along the way, the success we seek moves farther from us. When we honor ourselves by taking our bodies and minds seriously, we have the opportunity to bring closer the things we wish to manifest. Success starts, happens, and ends where it was conceived, within!

THE TWENTY (TO TWO) MINUTE JOURNEY TO TAP INTO *YOUR* CERTAINTY

Please don't be a perfectionist. This is about you. Practice. Experience. Let yourself learn about yourself, and really enjoy finding out what's available to you, from you.

1. Body Awareness. 10 minutes.

Look at yourself in a large mirror, preferably a full-length mirror, without wearing too many baggy clothes that will mask your stance. Look. What do you see? Don't get critical. Just look to see what your body looks like, posture-wise. (Skip the "need to fix this and that.") Look at your posture. Look for tension. Then, stop paying attention to the image in the mirror and simply feel what it's like to be in your body. How does your body feel from the outside in? Become aware of points of stress: neck, shoulder, rib cage, back, pelvis. Feel your tongue as it rests in the bed of your jaw. Feel your forehead. Feel your feet hit the floor. Feel how your hands fall away from your wrists. Then, observe how your body changes posture and position as you become more present and aware.

2. Breath Awareness. 5 minutes.

Stand or sit comfortably in a quiet space. Listen to your own breath. Observe how your body moves slightly as you take in and let out your air. Begin to exaggerate your breath, so it sounds like Darth Vader from Star Wars, but don't force it. Listen to the powerful inhale and exhale. After a few rounds, let your breath settle again to a more quiet state. Notice how your mind becomes quiet as you stay present observing the sound of your breath.

3. Welcome Your Inner Voice. 5 minutes.

In the few moments following the first two steps of this exercise, your level of distraction will be minimized. It's a good time to let your inner wisdom speak up. You won't have to try to find it. It will find you, and more likely than not it will give you some insight you'll find valuable. Don't be shy if you'd like to verbalize a question. Do it. If you don't get a message or insight the first time (or at any other time), be patient, and just enjoy the momentary bit of equanimity in your mind and body.

Once you get used to perceiving how your body feels and what a normal, balanced breath is like, you can practice tapping into your own certainty in about two minutes. Plan on doing this exercise daily until it becomes natural to do it anytime. As your awareness becomes more keen, you will find it easier and quicker to execute wherever you are. In the meantime, give yourself about either 30 days or 30 tries before you make any judgment. Remember, you created your own vision and it came from within. Tap into that magical place to help it manifest just the way you'd like.

About Dr. Amelia

Amelia is an expert in integrative medicine and natural health care solutions who, since 1990 has been advocating safer and more effective solutions than drugs to help people minimize pain and improve poor body function. Her business, Universal Health Institute, is the cornerstone of integrative health care in Chicago, and her entrepreneurial spirit has been honored as an award winner for *Make Mine a Million* as well as Goldman Sachs *10,000 Small Businesses*. Amelia is known for creating a business that focuses on looking further than just getting rid of a health problem, asking, "Okay, now how do we boost your immunity, get you stronger, build your energy, and help you manifest a better state of health and well being?" Amelia has been a guest clinician on NBC, and a host of "We Are Concerned", a public television show bringing alternative health care advice to Chicagoans. She has also been featured in *Today's Chicago Woman, Crain's Chicago Business* and *The Chicago Sun Times* as a businesswoman and expert in health care.

In addition to being a featured clinician on the cover of *The American Chiropractor*, Amelia has been featured in CNNs Headline News anchor Robin Meade's New York Times best-selling book (*Morning Sunshine*, Center Street Publishing) that highlighted how she helped Robin overcome panic attacks by using the Demartini Method, a non-drug method to improve mental health. Amelia continues to lecture at a variety of healthcare graduate school programs on integrative care including schools throughout the U.S., the U.K., France, Holland and Belgium. While in Chicago, she spends her time working with patients and traveling to teach the local medical community about complimentary alternative health care choices for themselves and their patients. In the meantime, she continues to write her Business Books for Girls series, *Princesses With A Twist*.

To learn more about Dr. Amelia Case visit: www.uhichicago.com and www.drameliacase.com and www.princesseswithatwist.com

CHAPTER 17

The Art of Delegation

By Doreen Zayer

A while ago, I asked one of my managers to fire an employee. I was on vacation at the time, and the matter couldn't wait for my return.

As requested, the manager ended the staffer's employment, but not without some emotional strain on both parties.

In fact, the fired employee was so distraught, she saddened the manager, who later complained, "Do not ever ask me to fire someone again. It was awful!"

The emotional upheaval was resolved by re-hiring the terminated staff member.

This was clearly one of those times when the delegation of responsibility didn't produce the desired results.

Properly done, however, the "art of delegation" allows you to design your life, and offers those around you the opportunity to do the same.

Delegation can be an invaluable tool for enhancing the quality of your home life, business and general well-being.

WOMEN WHO MEAN BUSINESS

HOW TO BEGIN

There are very few tasks that cannot be delegated to another. The question is: How do you decide which responsibilities should be delegated, and which should not?

In addition, you will need to carefully weigh the skills and personality of the individual you are considering for the task.

To get started, think about all the things you do in the course of a typical day. Better yet, make a list of every daily task you perform for an entire week.

At the end of the week, decide which activities you enjoyed, and which ones you disliked, or worse – detested. Then, compile two lists:

1) Which tasks did I love doing?
2) Which tasks did I hate doing?

From these lists, create a category that identifies chores only you can do or would enjoy continuing; and a category for responsibilities you would like to pass along to someone else.

ASSIGN YOUR LEAST FAVORITES

Why not begin your delegation of responsibilities by first relinquishing tasks you'd rather not do in the first place?

This is where a worker's skill and disposition come into play. Before you assign a responsibility, consider the interests and talents of specific individuals. If you have employees or family members well-suited for a task, think about the benefits – monetary compensation, self-esteem or otherwise – they may receive from tackling it.

Even though a necessary chore may seem less than delightful to you, someone on your team likely can handle it and quite possibly enjoy their new responsibility.

PREPARE TO BE TESTED

Once delegated, parting with a chore may not be easy.

For example, I offered my teenage son $10 a week to take care of our cats, Oliver and Hershey.

This meant I would no longer be responsible for providing their essential needs, such as food, water and a clean litter box. But the transition didn't go as smoothly as expected.

Here's why: Although assigned, a former task will remain on your radar. It will return to you, test you, tease you and tempt you to pick it up again.

There may be legitimate reasons for you to resume the task on your own when you are not yet comfortable without it. In my case, I certainly wouldn't have sat idly by if Oliver and Hershey had been threatened with starvation. Daily tasks are habitual and we all know how hard it is to change our routines. In time, I got over it.

WE CAN'T DO EVERYTING

As business owners, many of us believe: "We can do it best; if it's meant to be, it's got to be me."

This is where I have an advantage: Experience has taught me that I don't know everything, and can't do everything as well as I'd like. I have learned when to seek, find, hire and replace myself with people who do specific things much better than I do.

The fine art of delegation is no more than:

- Accepting the fact that you can't do it all.
- Acknowledging that you don't enjoy all of your daily chores.
- Honing your ability to find others who are ready, willing and capable of rising to a new challenge and responsibility.

The result of well-executed delegation is priceless. The more responsibilities you successfully delegate, the more time you will have for new opportunities to enrich your day with moments that bring you joy.

PUT EGO ASIDE

You can be ego seduced into believing only you can do it right, get it done and produce the necessary results. But it doesn't need to be that way.

I worked with a business consultant who said, "All my clients want to see me, only me; and as I began to grow, they refused to work with any other consultants."

What did she do?

"I raised my fees," she said. "At the time, the fee for my employees' services was $250 an hour; I would tell them, 'so-and-so is available but if you really want to see me, the fee is $500 hourly.'"

The clients suddenly were willing to work with one of her endorsed consultants.

EMBRACING MOTHERHOOD AND BUSINESS

If you keep doing what everyone else wants you to do, how will you ever do what you want?

As mothers, we understand this very well. This is why the female entrepreneur has both an advantage and disadvantage in the world of business ownership.

We have the advantage of knowing that motherhood is our most important role, and as businesswomen, face the challenge of wrestling with the roughest time-management battle known to mankind.

When I began taking the steps toward business ownership -- writing a business plan, looking for locations and negotiating rents — I was pregnant.

It seemed natural for well-meaning people to say, "Don't you think you should focus on the baby? You have a 2-year-old and you're pregnant?"

Nowadays, I can laugh about it; but back then, doubt crept in and I wondered if I was doing something wrong, something against the pure nature of motherhood.

What kind of a mother would strut her big belly around a shopping mall, unless she was looking for maternity clothes? I did that and more, discussing the square-foot costs and common-area charges in various parts of the shopping center.

Things are as we perceive them to be. If you're OK starting a business when you're 17, 35, 55 or 85, who am I to try and dissuade you?

Yet, there are plenty of people in our lives who will offer us sound advice, contrary to our own entrepreneurial ambitions, because they truly believe it to be best for us and our families.

Fortunately, I put the warnings aside and continued my journey.

My kids are now 19, 16 and 9; and somehow they miraculously got there with all of their fingers and toes. It's me who's grey, worn and underpaid. I say this only for effect: I color my hair whatever I'm in the mood for; I wake up at 7 a.m. excited to begin a new day, and I love what I do at home and at "work" - at least, most of the time.

Negotiating rent for my first store in our only local mall wasn't nearly as challenging as arranging time to be home on weeknights, school nights, weekends and holidays. It's far more demanding to negotiate a satisfactory deal with a teenager than it is with a landlord.

A LESSON ABOUT LIFE

I remember when one of my sons was around 2 years old; I was pushing him on a swing and my dad was with me. I was obsessing about my new business.

I kept going on and on about the challenges of opening a new business – the rent, the electrician that did not show up, and on and on – until my dad gently said, "Your son is asking you something."

At that moment, like a slap across the face, I snapped back into the moment. I had stopped pushing the swing; my son was saying, "Look what I can do" as he hung above and swung from the frame of the swing.

He had shimmied up the chain and onto the tubular frame above, delighted in his agility and height. How easy it is to disappear into thought and task and remove us from the present moment.

I so cherish every moment with each of my children, at every age and stage, that when something pulls me away from them I have got to be handsomely rewarded.

I can remember before opening my business my first son was around a year old. I would take my travel massage-table to the New Jersey shore and work on a few people. The ride there was about an hour or more depending on traffic.

I would go from home to home. Some would be ready for me, and others not. Some clients wanted the table on the sand; this was not so good when the stress on my legs and the summer heat were considered, but I'd say OK just the same.

And some clients would complain about the price: "$50 dollars. Can't you do better than that? When Gloria comes she charges only $40. Why is it so much?"

I would coax him back into the moment of relaxing and he would pay the $50. I would usually see four people at the shore on a given day; $200 wasn't bad for a few hours of work. I would then drive home to see my beautiful son.

One morning, he was playing in a little blue plastic pool on our deck and I did not want to leave. I wanted to stay and enjoy this exact moment for as long as I could. But $200 beckoned, so I had to go.

And once again, the very same client challenged my fee of $50.

"Why so much? Gloria was here and she is only charging us $40 each?" he said.

I fanaticized responding with: "If I'm going to leave my baby and come all the way here, jackass, and move the table on and off the sand, in and out of four different houses and listen to you bitch about $10 every week, then damn it, you're going to have to make it worth my while."

My actual retort was a bit milder.

"Maybe you should continue working with Gloria," I said.

I never went back. Why? That experience brought me $200 but no joy.

The price of doing business cannot be allowed to rob us of our joy.

MASTERING THE ART OF DELEGATION

If you can't delegate some responsibilities to others you cannot enjoy all that you've worked to achieve.

Many business owners have a job that totally depends upon them all the time, everyday. It dictates everything else: Do I go to my son's basketball game, award ceremony and my daughter's talent show? Do I participate in this local fund-raiser? Can I speak at the young women's leadership conference?

So, how do you know when you have mastered "the art of delegation?"

I believe you know you have mastered "the art of delegation" when an employee you are prepared to fire quits of his or her own free will.

Complete mastery of delegating is when you do nothing and what needs to be done seemingly happens without effort. It is just the inevitable unfolding in front of you, with each individual performing what they need to do next.

Self-mastery – knowing when to stay with a task, when to let it go and when to move on – is reserved for both the business owner and each individual employee.

The art of delegation allows you to design your life and offers those around you the opportunity to do the same.

ABOUT DOREEN

In her home community of Staten Island, N.Y., Doreen Zayer has earned a well-deserved reputation for both philanthropic generosity and world-class business prowess.

Doreen, a former Peace Corps volunteer, launched her enterprise, Relax On Cloud Nine, in 1995 as a dollar-a-minute massage store in the Staten Island Mall. The modest venture has since grown into one of the largest and most respected businesses of its kind in the New York metropolitan area.

It has been highlighted in Time Out New York magazine as "homey, peaceful and unlike anything you can experience in Manhattan."

Concurrent with the growth of her enterprise, Doreen has continually supported her community, helping to raise money for local schools, houses of worship, and charitable and cultural foundations, such as Eden II, an organization that assists children with autism and their families; the Staten Island Zoo, and the Historic Richmond Town village and museum complex on Staten Island.

In 1997, just two years after starting her business, Doreen purchased a magnificent Victorian residence within the Staten Island neighborhood of West Brighton.

A year later, following extensive renovations and remodeling of the historic 1800s structure, she relocated Relax On Cloud Nine to its new luxurious home.

Upon arrival, Doreen's massage therapy endeavor embraced a wide range of additional top-notch services, transforming Relax On Cloud Nine into one of the most alluring and highly-touted day spas in New York City.

Today's visitors to Relax On Cloud Nine can opt for any number of pampering and wellness-inspired spa services, ranging from massages, facials, body scrubs and acupuncture to Vichy showers, sauna or steam showers, mud/seaweed wraps and air-brush tanning, to name just a few.

Over the years, Doreen has been recognized numerous times for her entrepreneurial accomplishments and community commitment, including such honors as:

The Staten Island Chamber of Commerce's Louis R. Miller Business Leadership Award (2010); American Express Open's Make Mine a $Million Business Award (2006); New York State Small Business Hall of Fame "Extraordinary Entrepreneurial Spirit" Award (2006); Small Business Development Center Hall of Fame (2005); Outstanding Women-Owned Small Business, presented by the Small Business Development Center at the College of Staten Island, City University of New York (2004).

Relax On Cloud 9 is located at 694 Clove Road, Staten Island, NY. 10310-2707. The spa may be reached by phone at 718-448-3412 and visited online at: www.relaxoncloud9.com. Doreen may be contacted directly via email at: doreen@RelaxOnCloud9.com.

CHAPTER 18

DON'T BE BITTER, BE BETTER!

By Maria Struik

Have you ever felt that you were being catapulted into a life-altering situation, without being able to do anything about it; a feeling of having lost control altogether? No way to steer your way out of this?

Well that happened to me when my husband was diagnosed with cancer and passed within two weeks, and all this, while John and I had become entangled in the legal battle of our lifetime, a battle for ultimate financial survival, stressed to the max.

We were a happy family, with me being a homeschooling Mom and business partner to my husband. Life was good and beautiful.

John had been the area franchisee for Northern Ontario (Canada) for an international food company for almost 30 years, when corporate ownership changed in 2006. John and I had always maintained a good and friendly relationship with the franchisees in our area, as we believed in helping whenever needed, for the greater good of all, always looking for a Win-Win situation.

When a franchisee encountered a challenge, my husband was always there, to advise or otherwise assist in whatever capacity needed. For years the company had expanded its number of units, not by taking huge amounts of kickbacks from supply purchases or by charging enormous royalty fees to the operators, but by being ingenious marketers and smart franchisors.

Within a few months after the corporate ownership change, we noticed the individual units drastically going down in profitability, some calling us that they couldn't make the lease payments, etc. At first we couldn't quite understand, but it wasn't long before we realized that the heavy rebate burden was literally choking each and every operator, unless the franchisee was prepared to sink his life savings into his operation as a temporary band-aid measure. It wasn't long before it came to a legal confrontation between corporate and John, in his capacity as the area franchisee.

Any of you familiar with the legal system, can appreciate how long it takes and how slow the system works. My husband and I wanted to help and ended up becoming victims, along with the franchisees, who lost either their restaurant or their life savings or both. Almost 2 years into this seemingly never-ending judicial mess, we received the worst news a family can receive:

You have cancer and there is no cure!

There was no time for John and me to plan an exit strategy, out of this legal swamp. John passed so quickly, way too quickly.

Suddenly and completely unexpectedly, I found myself in totally unfamiliar waters, without my stronghold and steersman, my husband, my John. I couldn't discuss these issues with anyone, as nobody but John would know the inside of it all. I felt lost, helpless and vulnerable; I was without bearings and without direction, when my very true friend and confidante, my Mother, passed away only 4 months after John. Please don't start believing that I had super human strengths to move through these personal tragedies, trust me I truly didn't. I did my share of crying (and still do).

I was looking to follow someone, something, when I came across a very profound statement made by Lee Milteer in an interview, where she talks about how she received this coffee mug from one of her friends. She says that it wasn't the mug that had made such an impression on her, but rather what it said on the mug.

It said: *Good Morning, this is GOD. I will be handling ALL your problems today. I will not need your help.*

That stuck with me, especially when every decisive action on my part was met with controversy from the opposition. Endless and relentless legal battles were my daily diet. You have heard them say: *If it doesn't kill you it makes you stronger!*

Well I must have become a lot stronger through all of this.

With Faith, the children, a few true friends, hard work and determination, I made it through to settlement number One. For about 3 months, corporate and I appeared to be speaking the same language, but before long, we again had to seek legal intervention, except this time, it was through arbitration. Another year went by, before we finally reached a buy-out arrangement, this after more than 5 years of court attendances, etc.

There was a little pause, maybe a week. I couldn't really believe that I wouldn't be involved in John's company anymore, but I enjoyed the thought of being able to spend more time with the children as I wouldn't have to travel all over Northern Ontario anymore. I actually started liking the idea of taking time off to plan my future, perhaps a new career in a different field.

But this didn't last long. As John and I held most of the leases on the franchises within our area, I had taken care of ensuring the payments to the Landlords. It was my lawyers' as well as my own belief that corporate would insist on taking these Leases on, themselves, as all of them housed or had housed a franchise.

Not so! When I offered corporate these Leases at no charge to them, they didn't want the Leases. Now, there was no choice left for me, other than to generate the Lease payments somehow. After consulting with my legal team and after reviewing my buy-out agreement to avoid a conflict in that regard, I brain-stormed ideas for a new venture in the hospitality industry. As I am writing this chapter, a new lawsuit has been commenced by the same corporate individual; based on the non-compete (non-competition) section of my settlement!

1. There was no time to develop a strategy or a letter of conduct; a how-to-do-list or even a class one could attend to study how to deal with this. Like in real life, you have to learn as you go. I discovered that <u>you can't lead when you follow.</u>

I love this Chinese proverb: Mend the first break, kill the first snake, and conquer everything you undertake! I think it sort of applies to my circumstances and how I had to adapt to the hand we were dealt. Sink or swim!

2. I am starting to adopt <u>an attitude of gratitude</u>, to say "Thank You" more often, even for small or seemingly meaningless things. (It actually helps oneself to think for a moment about the gift or the help received.)

I have developed a new way to look at every situation; as to either what I have learned from it or what my life lesson is supposed to be, i.e., what am I to take away from this challenge or situation.

3. We business people all need and want to work on our brand these days; my advice is to always stay true to what your brand is all about. You are your brand. Never sacrifice your or your brand's integrity. <u>Integrity and personality must be cornerstone values.</u> Develop these values, cultivate them and always stay true to them. (Remember, you are ultimately accountable to the person looking back at you in the mirror.)

4. It is through persistence and perseverance that we move from stage to stage in our life and in our career. A lot of times we ourselves don't just realize how strong we are

and can be under very challenging circumstances. But <u>by being focussed</u> on what you want to accomplish or need to do, one is often surprised at one's own achievements and strengths. We were all born with this inner power, with this deep source of unimaginable energy to survive.

5. <u>Be determined and stand by your words.</u> It is more important to be respected than to be liked. Face it, more often than not you feel like the lone voice in the wilderness. I have become used to liking that lonely feeling; the way out there; perhaps almost insane statements and ideas, because that is where it is less crowded. That is where opportunity awaits you.

6. I have made it my mission to always <u>underpromise and overdeliver,</u> whether that is with the guests in our restaurants or with the franchisees in our organisation. It is in all our marketing: We want to WOW you!

In business, you need to develop a "<u>war room mentality,</u>" being always on high alert. Being on the lookout for where your competitors are heading is a good defense strategy. Keeping an eye on your employees is like protecting against espionage during a time of war.

Absolutely treat everyone with the highest respect, but do not blindly trust anyone. Ponder the old saying: keep your friends close and your enemies even closer.

Another part of our "war room mentality" is to be always dressed for action, by that I am not referring so much at the literal interpretation as much as at the figurative meaning. Try to look on the bright side of things and radiate your positive energy; it has an amazing impact on the people and the world around you. Problems and challenges become easier to handle when there is positive energy in the air. People are more upbeat in that type of environment. I think of this often when I enter one of our restaurants to speak to management and staff; put on your 'positive' hat; it has a profound impact. Besides that, if we emit positive energy, we look better and (much) younger.

7. <u>Trust your inner voice</u>. Most of the time that voice is right on the money. You can *FEEL IT.* In every deal, the customer is king and everyone is important, but do not waste your time, if you *FEEL* that the deal or the transaction is not going to materialize, politely bow out, quickly. As Zig Ziglar said: *There is a customer born every minute.* Time is a non-renewable resource and you have only one life, make it count! (You can't make $100K a year doing $10/hour jobs.)

As a team, we hold strong to the <u>philosophy of sharing</u>. We share our knowledge, we share our ideas and we share profitability so that we all grow stronger. Keep in mind: sharing knowledge does not make you less smart. I try to show my team by example rather then by indoctrination, as to how I like my brand supported. I mean we do need both, but more by example, as that shows who I am. I believe that it is extremely important to focus on people's strengths and not be down on them about their weaknesses. There is hardly anything worse than to be treated in a condescending manner. Respect is the key and foundation to any long-term relationship. As a teamleader, you shouldn't have to micro-manage; *empower your people.* Give your people the opportunity to impress you. People love to belong to something bigger than themselves. Allow them to shine, because it will also look great on you.

Another very important aspect to teamwork is: <u>listening</u>! My Mom always reminded us that there was a reason God gave us two ears and one mouth. If you want to lead a successful company, life or partnership, you need to listen twice as much as you speak. Other people have great ideas too! Be grateful if they want to share them with you (and your company).

As I have come to grow a little more comfortable in my new role as an entrepreneur, I don't feel a sense of pride or accomplishment, but I feel rather humbled by the opportunity given to me. An opportunity to help business partners and clients in achieving their highest potential in their respective fields. At the same time, this opportunity also places an undeniable obligation on me to give the best I can, in all aspects, and to be the best I can be.

I don't think that we are ever done learning, or teaching and sharing. The minute you think that you know it all or have heard it all, you closed your mind; in effect, you are dead to the world around you.

We are all a work in progress, and we need to remember that every minute of the day so that we practice a little patience with ourselves as well as with others. Ultimately, it is not about you or me, but about our brand, about what we are standing for in life, what we are leaving as a legacy and about what we are doing to make and leave our world a better place.

About Maria

With more than 25 years of experience in the hospitality industry, Maria Struik is a natural in this very demanding and always changing business.

Maria was educated in the Netherlands. Upon immigrating to Canada, she went back to school to obtain her Real Estate and Business Brokers License. After meeting her late husband John, who was an Area Franchisee for an international food franchise, they worked as a husband and wife team. Their employment as Area Franchisees was a job which they both enjoyed tremendously, as it was a combination of hospitality and real estate, meeting and helping people of all walks of life. John's sudden passing 3 years ago, and ongoing legal confrontations with the new corporate ownership led to a settlement, which left Maria with no other alternative than to re-think the hospitality industry as a whole.

Maria understands all too well how busy everyone's life is these days; how we all long to think back of the time when Mom made delicious home-cooked meals. (Remember the stack of pancakes with real Log Cabin Syrup, or the delicious bowl of fresh-made soup?)

This is what inspired Maria to redevelop a concept, which provides the old familiar foods in a more contemporary setting -- "smothered" with hospitality, second to none. The long familiar and proven diner concept was renamed Roosters Diner. Maria is responsible for overseeing the existing units, as well as site selection and recruitment of new operators.

Maria is an active Pro-Life member and likes to help rather than to criticize. One of her goals is to establish a training school in hospitality. She wants to offer special opportunities and incentives for attendance to expectant mothers, thereby providing training and a career choice. She hopes that this will help these mothers-to-be to find employment after giving birth.

For the past two years, Maria has been a finalist in the North American Marketing Contest. Just recently, she was named Cambridge Who's Who Entrepreneur of the Year in the Hospitality Industry. While inclusion in the Cambridge Who's Who Registry is an honor, only a small selection of members in each discipline are chosen for this distinction.

To learn more about Roosters Diner and how you can become involved in this not-so-ordinary new concept, please call:

Toll Free: 1-866-973-9013

Or visit: www.roostersdiner.com

CHAPTER 19

How To Attain Your Dreams: Are You a D.I.V.A. or A.V.I.D.?

By Michele Rohde

Have you ever wondered why some people seem to have it all? …Success! …Money! …Happiness! Well, there could be a myriad of reasons behind having a wealth of those things. However, for the common person who didn't receive a trust fund, a happy pill, a winning lotto ticket or some other rare or unnatural circumstance, I believe they came by their success, money and happiness because they have minimal fear, and refuse to make excuses in the face of adversity. That's it. I think that's the common denominator among the group of people that live in abundance of success, money &/or happiness. I've come to be convinced of this through several of my own personal and business experiences and through those of others.

Jumping off into a risk headfirst is something my husband and I have become known for, and even labeled as crazy a time or two. And believe me, those ventures haven't come without lessons. One thing I have found in ALL of the risks we've taken, and for many others, is that we had minimal fear. We knew exactly what we wanted, and we were PASSIONATE about it! We'd find a way around any risks (always legally and ethically, of course), or suck it up if we couldn't. Sure, we'd have our moments worrying over decisions (because doing the right thing keeps us up at night), but for the most part, if you had asked us to abandon our dream, we'd call YOU crazy! And, we've probably annoyed so many people over the years talking about our dreams: starting a new business, building another home, getting married at 18, a baby at 30, etc., etc. But I believe this is part of what contributes to success – sharing your dreams – which I'll go into more detail later.

Something else I've noticed is that we despise excuses from ourselves or others, and don't enjoy hearing the words "No" or "Can't." That, coupled with seeing the world through rose-colored glasses and being naively optimistic, can lead to immensely great or dangerous ends. Luckily for us, we had friends and family members who had successes and made mistakes before us, so we were able to soundboard and learn. I'm not trying to toot my own horn here, because we are far, far from perfect (and have made many mistakes), but what I am trying to do, is relay to you what has worked for me in my life – removing the many things that haven't. All I try to do is repeat the positive as often as I can remember, and when I fall off the track (as I often do), something will call me to become passionate about a new vision, and off we go again! So here it is, my personal goal is for people, especially women, to become less afraid of all things money; how to save it, protect it, invest it, spend it and talk about it with my no frills, all-it-takes-to-have-more-of-what-you-want, less excuses and less fear approach.

Well, that seems simple enough. If all it takes to have positive things start to happen for you, and more of the things you want, is to decide not to be afraid and to not make excuses, then you're in! Right? Boy, do I wish it was that simple, but I've also come to learn the hard way, more than once, most things worth having are not obtained easily. So how do you take those common denominators and make something great happen for yourself, again and again?

I don't want to pretend I have a magic formula that is guaranteed to make you a millionaire, or promise to help you find your true love all within a year's time, but what I do have is a method I created for myself that has simply worked for me, time and time again. It is a formula I've shared with others that worked for them as well. I can hope, at best, that it does positive things for you too, if you choose to implement it with minimal fear and excuses. Here it is, my goofy acronym that has amazingly powered me through my own projects, dilemmas and life in general: Being a D. I.V.A.!

Yep, corny, I know! But I love it, and it works! So that's all that matters. This acronym and what it stands for had the power to help me achieve all of my goals over the years. Now I feel so naked! I just let my inner voice out and perhaps a pretty good secret. Well, now it's yours to know, and hopefully it helps you achieve your dreams, so let me finally define this crazy acronym for you and show you how it can help...

"D" is for delegate

"I" is for initiate

"V" is for values and

"A" is for accountability

Disclaimer: I felt comfortable with the word "Diva," but if you're a male or female that isn't, you can use "A.V.I.D." the same way instead.

So why did this help me so much? ...for a number of reasons. For starters, I connected with the word "DIVA" for the positive connotations it possesses – a powerful, in-charge woman who could do and have anything. That felt pretty good to me. Try it on! Walk around in it! Start thinking of yourself as a DIVA and see how YOU feel. Now, don't get too carried away! You don't want to use it as an excuse to abuse common courtesy and self-respect, but use the label in a positive, empowering way. If you've been demanding green M&M's at every event you're invited to, you are officially abusing your DIVA powers! So, now that you are wearing your new positive and powerful DIVA inner-wardrobe, let me explain further how this word can help you.

Let's start with what you want or need. What is it that you don't yet have? What do you need help with? Is it a new job, a new house, an education, a savings account, a partner, or some other personal or business goal? Whatever your goal is, you need to clearly define it. This is your first step before you can truly become a DIVA. How do you clearly define a goal? Well, if you don't already have one, go grab a fun journal at the local dollar store and write down your goal on the first page. Make sure it also has a timeline and a dollar amount, if applicable. Let me give you some examples:

Examples of Well-defined Goals:

- My husband and I would like to build our first home costing approximately $300,000 within the next three years, so we want to save $60,000 for a down payment within that time frame.

- I would like to find a job in the field of healthcare within four months, paying no less than $45,000 a year with benefits, and within 30 minutes of my home.

Examples of Ill-defined Goals:

- I want to save money for an emergency.

- My fiancé and I want to start a real estate business.

The well-defined goals are good because they are very specific with timelines, dollar amounts and other details. The poorly-defined goals are lacking all of those characteristics. If you were going to bet money, who would you bet on succeeding? …The people with the defined or undefined goals? Studies have shown that those individuals who take the time to clearly define their goals and then actually write them down have a much higher chance of achieving those goals. So that is where you begin. After you have your goal(s) defined and written down in a place you can easily refer to, then you can pull out that DIVA acronym and get busy!

Remember what "D" stands for? **Delegate.** Why is delegating important? These days, time is limited and time is money, so the less time you have to spend working on something you want, the more time you have to focus on maximizing your efforts and, if it's done correctly, hopefully keeping more money in your pocket as well. So what am I talking about here? Look at your goal. (And remember, we only want to attempt one goal at a time at first, until you really get the hang of it; then you can try to tackle several at a time once you've mastered the process. If you have more than one goal right now, narrow it down to one by prioritizing by level of importance.) Start with your #1 goal.

What needs to be done to accomplish this goal? Write these tasks down – all of them. And be specific. It won't help you much to breeze through any of these steps. The more time you devote to this project, the better off you'll be. If you get stuck not knowing what exactly you need to do to accomplish your goal, don't fret…I haven't met anyone yet that was born with all the answers! The answers don't have to remain a mystery though. Information is just arm's length within reach. What you want to do is find an expert in the field of your goal and ask questions until it hurts. You could also research the answers on the Internet, but this may take longer than asking someone with experience. For example, if you want to save money for a specific goal, you may want to seek the opinion of a financial advisor. If you want advice on real estate, speak to a builder or a realtor. If you've recently lost a spouse through divorce or death, reach out for help if you have financial or other questions – you don't have to figure it all out yourself.

Get a second opinion for good measure. Keep in mind that you always have veto power too, and can say "no" or "I'll think about it" to anything that doesn't feel right. Then write down those tasks that you've gathered which are the most important to accomplish. Once you have your checklist, take a closer look at what can and can't be delegated. You don't necessarily want to spend all of your hard-to-come-by time on all of these items, so who can help you and what are the costs, if any? Delegate what makes sense economically and time-wise. Don't forget, if you are married, or have a partner, you can even delegate tasks to them so you don't have to shoulder all of the weight! If you are saving for your child's education, and after calculations, it's decided you need to save $250 a month for 10 years, you could each save $125 from each paycheck – delegate. Or if you are working on a business venture, the partner that has more people skills could work on sales tasks, while the partner with the book smarts could work on the paperwork – all examples of efficient delegating. Remember, there are a lot of professionals out there too in various fields that will give good advice at no charge. Ask around, then delegate to them if it makes sense.

Now that you've delegated part of your list, we're on to the letter "I" for **Initiate.** This is where you come in. The pieces that you couldn't delegate, you need to OWN! These are your babies and you can't drop them! You need to commit to accomplishing these tasks and envision a drill sergeant, a really intimidating one preferably, barking and breathing down your neck until you accomplish them. If you put yourself under a healthy amount of pressure to complete your items, you will feel such an amazing sense of accomplishment, you'll want to do it again. Don't forget to have a mini-victory dance or some similar cheap celebration when you do accomplish your tasks.

Once you've decided what items are yours to initiate, you need to "check yourself" and make sure you have letter "V" involved. "V" is for **Values.** If your goal isn't backed up by your underlying values, your chances of accomplishing it are reduced. You don't want that because you could easily lose steam in the midst of working toward a goal. That's a lot of time you don't want to waste. Let me give you another example; let's say you decide you want a boat. If the motives for wanting a boat aren't for the right reasons (such as to impress others), you may wake up in the process and realize it's not worth the effort, and you could already have lost time and money. But let's say, you decide you want a boat because it will afford you quality time with your family doing an activity everyone loves. Well then, you've identified a value that is important to you that is tied to this goal, which thereby again increases your odds of achieving this goal. Please make sure you don't skip this part of the process either thinking it is silly or assuming your goal is already a value of yours. Devote the time to ensuring that your goal is relative to your underlying values – double check yourself, and then of course, write your value down too.

The last letter in the DIVA acronym is "A" for **Accountability.** This, in my opinion, is the most important part in goal setting. Tell everyone!! The more people you tell about your goal, the better. It's been proven, like the other techniques, to improve your odds of success, but I believe it also helps you achieve your goal in quicker time. I think it does this for a few reasons. Number one, it makes you very accountable. You probably value the opinions and respect of those closest to you, as do I, so you want to make them proud. If you tell your goal to those people, the ones closest to you first, you won't want to let them down, so you're going to try harder to get to your goal. The second, and perhaps more interesting thing that happens, is people might start trying to actually help you achieve your goal when you reveal it. This is very cool! People who love you will want to help you. And this may surprise you, but even some strangers will want to help you. So share, share away!

If you fully commit to this process, I believe you will see many positive changes in yourself and your surroundings. Please remember throughout the process though, that this is all about improvement, not perfection. Give yourself permission to hit the "restart" button if you need to. Don't beat yourself up about anything, …and have fun with it. I know once I started acting more like "Ally McBeal," the more fun I had with sometimes not-so-fun topics. (If you don't remember this character from the sitcom, she used to have elaborate, very entertaining, running dialogues in her mind.) So what I am saying is, since I didn't start out born with confidence, I had to create an *alter ego* – kinda like Beyoncé did. Ha!! I've accomplished nothing compared to mega-talented Beyoncé, but what I find intriguing is I've heard Beyoncé say in several interviews, that she has an alter-ego by the name of "Sasha Fierce" and when she goes on stage, "Sasha" takes over and gives her the confidence to sing to thousands upon thousands, and dance like you've never seen! I'm sure this same act is true among many who have seen success. There really is something to the old cliché, "Fake it till you make it," which I happen to love and lived by in the infant stages of my career – as I mentally called myself the "DIVA of the Dollar!" to encourage inner confidence in the fact that I knew what I was doing and could do it well. You can do the same thing in the process of reaching for YOUR dream! Once you've accomplished your goal, be sure, and this is super vital too, to reward yourself, even if its small or free, like a candle-lit dinner at home or an intimate get together with friends to celebrate the accomplishment they all knew you were working so hard toward. So, like I said earlier, put on your mental DIVA wardrobe and get busy!

About Michele

Michele Rohde is a financial advisor with a passion for helping the average Joe succeed in achieving all of their goals.

She graduated from the University of Houston - Victoria with a BBA, and is certified by the College for Financial Planning as an Accredited Asset Management Specialist.

Michele was honored to be voted "Best of the Best" of Financial Advisors by the Victoria Advocate, has been Top Ten in Client Service Excellence with her firm for several years, was chosen as Woman of the Year by the National Association of Professional Women and has been humbled to receive many other local and national honors.

She is proud to serve in many volunteer roles, including as a mentor and female recruiter for her firm and as President for her local American Business Women's Association chapter, which has grown to be the second largest in the nation. Michele is fearless when it comes to accomplishing her ambitions, and wants you to have that same relentless drive when it comes to fighting for your own goals.

Michele was born and raised in her small hometown of Victoria, TX where she currently resides with her husband and high school sweetheart, Rocky, and their baby girl, Lexi.

For more information on Michele, go to her website:
http://www.michelerohde.com

CHAPTER 20

Job Fit or Lack Thereof is Wreaking Havoc on the Global Economy

By Julie Moreland

"I don't understand why I feel so tired lately and really don't feel like going to work" is the thought running through Samantha's mind. You see "Sam," as she likes to be called, as you stand on a busy street corner watching 'People' rushing by here and there on their way to and from work. They're teachers, carpenters, nurses, brokers, programmers, sales reps or maybe job candidates pursuing a promising interview. Can you tell who is feeling inspired and engaged versus those that are simply going through the motions? Would you have guessed that Sam is one of the miserable ones and doesn't even realize why? Working 60-hour weeks, making decent money, but somehow unfulfilled.

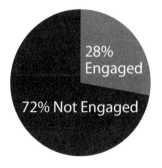

Sam is part of 72% of US workers who are not engaged in their work (Gallup).

How she ended up here is largely because of a system that's broken, but it's always been in various stages of 'broken' from the very beginning. Let's trace this one individual woman's steps. At 10 years old, Sam feels a passion for being a teacher and is fascinated by advertising. She has 'pretend' classrooms and dresses up her dogs for photo shoots with her friends. Then as a teenager, her friends seem to naturally flock to her for advice and to share their deepest thoughts on school, family and of course boys. At 16, Sam finds herself anxiously meeting with the high school counselor to tell her that she thinks she is interested in psychology. There is great dialogue and some interest surveys to fill out and a caring counselor who in their second meeting suggests that psychology may not the best fit. The counselor suggests that with Sam's great grades in math, maybe she should explore business…maybe become a CPA in fact because they are well respected professionals, make great money and don't have to deal with 'depressed' people all day. Sam leaves this session a little confused but excited to get started.

With some education and training under her belt, it appears that Sam does have a knack for business and excelled in all her business classes! She is enthusiastic and hopeful and is able to get a good job in finance with a respected company that appears to confirm that this is indeed a good path for her.

A couple of promotions later and in her mid 20's, she is 'making it' and making a reputation for herself. She has no idea what's about to change for her and why. One day, she wakes up and asks herself, "Why do I seem to feel so crappy all the time?" She is fatigued and just doesn't feel the enthusiasm she once did. She rarely sees her friends and family, and she can't remember the last time she had a day off. Reality sets in big time that something is very wrong…but what exactly? She's been so busy 'making it' that she is oblivious to anything else. Sam is depressed, disengaged and confused, and just going through the motions to get her job done.

What is really going on? Sam is unknowingly part of the $370 BILLION dollar loss to the US economy caused by the lack of productivity from actively disengaged employees in the US alone (Gallup). Sam was a motivated and engaged worker who fell victim to a broken system and found herself in a poor fit and unable to provide positive productivity.

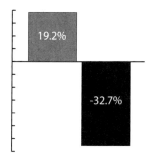

Companies with high levels of employee engagement improved 19.2% in operating income while companies with low levels of employee engagement declined 32.7% (Towers Watson).

The problem is that once people like Sam have paid hard-earned money for education and gained real world experience in a skill set, how do they just 'stop' doing that and start doing something else? Many people cannot afford to downgrade their pay and switch careers.

We can see the obvious problem for Sam as an individual, but what are other issues this broken system of 'trying on jobs' creates? Well the company that employs Sam has put time and money into grooming her for a career for which they are not likely going to see a long term return on their investment, because Sam will not be able to keep up this pace. She is likely to leave or if she stays, she may contribute to a statistic such as the fact that engaged employees in the UK take an average of 2.69 sick days per year; the disengaged take 6.19 (Gallup). This is a huge impact on Sam's team as often they see the lack of fit and when management doesn't act, this is toxic to the engagement level of the team itself. She may contribute to the statistic that 18% of dis-engaged employees actually undermine their co-workers' success (Gallup). But there are other impacts. The family that Sam is a part of likely does not get Sam's attention as before, because she is tired. She feels trapped in a job that is too demanding and she buries herself in it, because she wants to succeed. The community that Sam is a part of does not get the benefit of Sam's time and energy, because she actually has to work more hours just to keep up the pace of doing work that is not suited to her…it's a bad "fit". Everyone is impacted…Sam, her employer, her team, her family, her community and ultimately, the economy.

Let's explore this issue of "Fit." What does that mean?

Let's trace Sam through the process. When Sam first entered the job market there were plenty of jobs to apply for and she didn't have a difficult time getting interviews. Her personality stood out in interviews versus fellow accounting types who tended to be a little more reserved and conservative. She filled out job applications and went through interviews. The interviews were unscripted and some questions weren't legal, but neither Sam nor the interviewer knew it at the time. Sam was hired because of her positive and engaging <u>attitude</u> in the interviews and she had the required education.

After a couple of years on the job, Sam is working hard and getting great reviews and feedback for her work ethic and applies for a supervisor job along with other department employees. Sam was promoted based on her positive and engaging <u>attitude</u>, her work ethic and rapidly-growing <u>experienced skill set</u> in finance. Now Sam finds herself managing a department of 14 accountants.

Two years into the management job, Sam finds herself working 60-hour weeks consistently along with a long commute to and from work. She is struggling to acquire management skills the hard way…'trying different approaches' in running meetings, performance management, discipline and leadership of her department. Sam is rapidly feeling like she's missing something… but what? She feels like she is a better 'fit' for management than she was in a pure finance/accounting job, but she's working too many hours and unclear as to what to do to get a handle on things. In 2010, the 'average' spending of $682 per learner (Bersin & Associates) hardly suggests that companies are 'tooling' their 'people' with real skills.

After several years of the highest levels of stress Sam can recall, she is just too tired to fight to stay in the game. She becomes one of the statistics of the employees that are voluntarily quitting their job and <u>surpassing</u> the number of employees who are fired or discharged. (Statistics from February, June and October of 2010 - US Bureau of Labor Statistics)

Back in the job search market, Sam starts to do a great deal of research online, takes some career assessments and finds herself interested in the same things she was in high school such as psychology, management and marketing. This is common for many people to come full circle. Not only does Sam find herself seeking a career where she has no education or experience, but she also finds that the process itself has completely changed with the trend of social networking and personal branding, making it nearly impossible to get noticed! She asks herself, *"What do I do with CareerBuilder, LinkedIn, Facebook and BranchOut? Where do I start?"*

Sam updates her resume, signs up for LinkedIn, reaches out to her personal network, updates her profile and sets out on the journey of applying for jobs. After months of this, now she 'needs' a job, so she is applying for anything that is remotely close to what she wants.

After literally reading and researching hundreds of companies, checking ratings on Glassdoor, hundreds of online applications, thousands of hours meticulously filling out forms and taking tests, Sam is disheartened to find that rarely does she hear anything or get any sort of update from these employers. She is one of 13.9 million unemployed people in the US (BLS) alone and who typically fall into the proverbial 'black hole' of the online candidate experience. This black hole is becoming a well-known issue, but what is the hidden one?

Thanks to 100 Million LinkedIn Users (LinkedIn), more than 750 Million Facebook users (Facebook) with 50% of them logging on in any given day, these 'consumer candidates' can instantly share their experiences. They can find comfort commiserating with statements on Facebook, Twitter, LinkedIn, Glassdoor and other social communities such as "don't bother shopping at that store, because the way they treat people is a joke." So we not only have millions of people out of work, but they are having poor candidate experiences effectively creating a team of poorly treated consumers who are out evangelizing the negative attributes of your company.

Sam's story ends with her having a full time job of trying to find 'any' job and not able to provide her expertise, 'production' to our economy, and negatively sharing her experiences with hundreds of employer brands.

What can we take away from this story? We saw that in the beginning of Sam's journey, there was not good information available to her or her counselors to help her see that financial-type positions were not a fit for her behavioral competencies. The leadership positions were a good behavioral fit, but she did not have the skills and experience. In both cases, she had a great attitude and level of engagement. She was too burned out in the management role by the time she or anyone else noticed that she needed support to learn the skills. She then falls victim to the proverbial 'black hole' of the candidate experience as she tries to move into a better fit.

So what are some action steps we can take to impact this tragic reality we are facing as "People"?

If you are an employer who is hiring, some of the key action items are:

1. Define jobs concisely with quantifiable terms (review every year):

   a. Define 'success' by looking at current employees. How do you 'know' if they are being successful? Something has to be measured and defined.

   b. Use a valid behavioral assessment to create a benchmark for success that shows a proven track record of what behavioral competencies work in your environment, management style and specific jobs.

   c. Define the "KSA's" - What skill sets and experience has proven to be the most successful in our positions?

Replace generalities like 'must be a team player' with specifics like 'must continually collaborate with a 5-person team and maintain an 80% or higher customer satisfaction rating'.

2. Make sure your screening process covers three key areas in terms of "fit". First - Attitude & Level of Engagement, second - Skills & Experience, and third - Behavioral Competency. Most processes only 'actually' cover one or two of these. (Note: when hiring entry level jobs, most of your candidates are right out of school and don't have experience yet, so you HAVE TO make sure you at least have the other 2 components to make good decisions.)

❶ Attitude & Engagement (Company Fit)
What are the individual's attitudes toward work and work-related issues? Using assessments, behavioral interviews and 360 degree surveys, measure counter-productive behaviors that might affect their ability to be a productive employee.

❷ Personality & Cognitive (Job Fit & Development)
What are the individual's personality characteristics and cognitive abilities? Using assessments and behavioral interviews, measure job fit as well as determine areas for coaching, development and leadership.

❸ Skills & Experience (Job Fit & Development)
What level of skills does the individual have for various job related tasks? Using demonstrations and skills tests, assess their level of skill for particular job related tasks.

(PeopleClues)

3. How much does your company spend to get "eye-balls" on your company, product or service? Imagine your candidates are your potential 'customers' who in turn will help you make sure your process provides a good candidate experience! This is your marketing opportunity that most companies totally miss! Your process should be automated as much as possible and let candidates know where they are in the process and do something for them to help them in their career search. Provide tips, even coupons to your products/ services and anything you can in your emails, online application process to help them! You can actually provide them automated feedback on 'job fit' or lack thereof, which is the greatest gift you can give them for truly finding a job that is a good fit in the future.

4. Make sure your screening process is efficient, because every minute spent by your staff is precious and not scalable! Utilize technology to educate prospective employees, gather and organize information and communicate with those prospective employees about where

they stand in your process. Spend your 'labor' time of precious minutes with individuals who rise to the top of the heap with the best overall fit, and then choose between those using your behavioral interviews. Remember to keep this technology "SIMPLE"! There are lots of choices in the market for applicant tracking, assessments and background check services. Look for inexpensive and simple solutions for your hiring managers to use.

Why do we care? With a $370 BILLION annual loss to the US economy alone and 72 % of employees dis-engaged (Gallup), we see that Sam is representative of a valuable person who is unable to contribute a high level of productivity to an employer, herself, her family or community.

Job Fit and the candidate experience are wreaking havoc on our corporate profitability and level of engagement. There are some basic steps we can take to do our part and do better at matching people with jobs and leadership styles within our organizations. Our global economy is at stake!

About Julie

Julie Moreland is President of PeopleClues. As President of PeopleClues, Julie is responsible for leading the organization to meet global objectives. During the past 21 years, Julie has become a nationally-respected authority on practical business applications of assessment technologies.

As a high-level manager in a $5 billion, 160-branch division of a Fortune 100 company, Julie gained a perspective on the complex workings of a major corporation. She then ventured into the challenging world of high tech entrepreneurs as the CFO of a $4 million start up computer-solutions company.

Julie is the co-developer of several employment assessment products used by thousands of clients globally. These assessments are used for measuring job fit, attitude and level of engagement of candidates and employees. These assessments are built for pre-employment screening, career development, team development as well as training and development. Julie was recently successful leading an international team of Psychologists through a 3-year rigorous review and awarded an industry-coveted certification from the British Psychological Society for the PeopleClues Assessments. To end-user clients, this test registration gives peace of mind through the knowledge that the assessments they are using have been built to quality standards and have received an internationally recognized "seal of approval."

Julie holds a bachelors degree in Finance from the University of West Georgia with a secondary emphasis on Business Information Systems. As a Fellow of the Workforce Stability Institute, she has written a chapter of their flagship book, *How to Attract, Optimize and Hold your Best Employees.* Julie has recently been selected to co-author the forthcoming book "Women Who Mean Business" along with other leading women in business from around the world, to be published by CelebrityPress in June of 2012. Julie is also a member of the prestigious Women's President's Organization, a non-profit organization of presidents and CEOs of multimillion-dollar businesses.

Julie is currently focused on designing and promoting programs for improving the "Candidate Experience" and promoting best practices to encourage and assist companies in becoming a "Candidate Champion." She was also recently selected as an expert blogger for FastCompany.com where her blogs will be a regular series on Fast Company's Leadership page.

CHAPTER 21

A PERFECTIONIST IS FORCED TO DELEGATE

AND THE LESSONS LEARNED ABOUT HOW LETTING GO WILL SET YOU FREE!

By Katie Hughes, PhD

Delegation made it possible for me to create a successful business while working full time and achieving great things at my "real job." Yes, starting a manufacturing company while working sounds unlikely, but it is possible as long as you think about the market you are going to enter, the essential role you play, how money comes in and goes out, what needs to be done to keep customers happy, and *most importantly that YOU don't try to do everything.*

After finishing my doctorate in Chemistry from Princeton University, I took a job in a highly selective company in a management development program. There were three components of my job: managing people, managing the work that the department did, and improving the department or company by coming up with and *successfully implementing* creative solutions that improved the department or company's performance. It was not an easy job and results were expected in very short time frames. I enjoyed the work and challenges that the job provided, but then, like many over-achievers of my generation, I felt I could take on more.

On top of this job, I had a dream of starting a company to manufacture a product that I would sell to people who enjoyed dancing: Slip-On Dancers™. Slip-On Dancers™ fit over your shoes and allow you to twist and turn on hard wood or even carpet when you were wearing regular sneakers while reducing the risk of twisting knee injuries. I knew that many people from line dancers, to swing dancers, to people who loved Latin dance or any of the booming dance fitness classes would love my product! They wouldn't twist their knees when they tried to turn wearing regular shoes.

Soon after we began selling, my husband and I found ourselves filling orders before work in the morning and then I had to answer emails and phone messages for the business during lunch breaks at my regular job. In the evening, I spent time on the financials and the website maintenance. My husband and I had no down time together and, while we were making money, I was basically running myself ragged trying to return phone calls during my lunch break and answer emails quickly enough to provide acceptable customer service. Even though my company didn't have all that many orders, we were at capacity.

I had two options:

1) I could quit my full-time, good-paying job so that I could answer the company emails myself, fill the orders, and do all of the other the big picture things that the business required.

OR

2) I could hire someone to help me.

What I found was that, when forced into delegating tasks to which you add little or no basic value, the company tends to grow because a very valuable resource (your time) is freed up and put to better use.

The first step for me was to hire a virtual assistant who, with some training, was as good, if not better than me at handling customer issues and taking orders. Although I had to pay the assistant, we got more orders because of the marketing efforts I was then able to spend my time on, and I was able to then spend my weekends and free time adding value in other ways to my business, or even take a little time for myself.

I come from a family of women who will take on as much, if not more, than they can handle. We tend to act as if asking someone else to do "your" work is socially frowned upon, like admitting defeat. I think many women would identify with this feeling.

It took me a while to realize that I had bigger goals in mind, and that, if I wanted my business to grow, I simply had to value my time enough not to take on small tasks. In other words, I had to grow personally to get over that hesitation to let go and delegate.

As the business grew and I continued to reach my limit, I delegated any task that was not a key/high priority as soon as I could.

I started to ask myself why was delegating such a hard thing for most people to accomplish? Did women have more difficulty than men at delegating? Are we just holding onto time-consuming tasks as a way of procrastinating on the more difficult, big-picture things? And most importantly, could you break delegation down into easy steps to get managers of all shapes and sizes who previously struggled with delegation to take the first steps?

THE TOP REASONS WE HESITATE TO DELEGATE

1. **The top reason business owners hesitate to let go is usually because it seems unnecessary to pay someone to do something when they could do it better themselves.**

The problem is that there are too many tasks that need to be done for you to do them all. You are needed on the high priority projects.

Your money paid to an assistant will be best spent if you delegate tasks with fairly short learning curves, but that take you a long

215

time to accomplish. Spend money to free up your own time so that your time can add the most to the business.

I know, I know, it's very tempting to save money and do everything yourself. I recommend a virtual assistant whom you pay by the hour instead of hiring a full-time assistant. Consider this assistant as an investment in your overall growth of the business, just like paying the fees to set up the website or retail location. Hand off the tasks that are repetitive and take a lot of your time.

2. It's impossible to hand a task or series of tasks off if they are a jumbled mess.

Think about your ultimate goal for the task to be accomplished and then create a series of steps that will accomplish it. Quite frankly, even if you don't eventually hand the task off, you will be more efficient if you take a few minutes and think about how to instruct someone else.

For more complicated tasks that require decision-making based on your brand values, be sure the delegee understands the "why" in your examples and be sure to give feedback that include the "why" and ultimate outcome you desire. Similarly, you can also use a dollar figure above which you expect to be contacted, but below which you expect them to be able to make their own decisions, based on the brand's values. For example, I have told my assistant to take care of our customers. I want our brand to be good for customer service. If she feels she needs to take extra steps, like including an extra pair of Slip-On Dancers^{TM} or giving free expedited shipping because of a mistake we made, unless that decision is going to cost the company more than \$10, I fully expect her to deal with the situation. At the end of each month, ask for a report showing the "exceptions" they made for the customer, and let them know that they did a good job or why you think they should have made a different decision.

WHY MUST YOU DELEGATE?

A cautionary tale: If you do all the tasks in the business, how can you take on new projects or take the time to do the important things only you can do, like market strategy planning and new product development? If you get sick and can't answer emails, what happens to customer service? You will be busy, busy, busy for the rest of your business life. That means no vacations and stress levels that are through the roof because you will ALWAYS have nagging small things hanging over your head.

1. If You Own Your Own Company, Your Time Is The Most Valuable.

Your time is most likely the most valuable in the company. Put a price on your time and track it for a week. Spend your time doing the things where you add the most value. It makes monetary sense for you to let go if you can pay someone else to accomplish the task at half what your theoretical hourly rate would be, and handing off the task frees you up to do more important work on your list or simply to have time that allows you to recharge and makes you more productive later on.

2. Even though you're the owner, there are tasks that other people really are better at than you.

Do you really want to spend your time figuring out how to do some obscure thing in Photoshop when you could pay someone else to edit the photos for you, not only getting the task done more quickly and freeing up your time, but with an end product that is probably better than what you would have come up with?

Similarly, there are probably tasks on your list that you really DON'T like to do, but that someone on your team would love to do. If you were to hand it off, they would be quicker at it and probably enjoy it and you would have rid yourself of a task that you did not enjoy in the first place.

OK - I GET IT. I NEED TO DELEGATE.
HOW DO I DO IT?

Give me specifics: How do I effectively delegate a task off?

Many people don't have experience handing a task off. Here's the deal:

a) Pick the right task for the right person. For example, a basic virtual assistant should be able to answer the company phone for example, but maybe they can't keep the books for you without extra training.

b) Ask them if they would be willing to take over responsibility for a task and communicate why you are choosing to delegate to them over other people.

c) Tell them exactly what you want (with written examples), the timelines for progress updates and the final product (very important), and lastly, what form the final product should take.

d) Tell them you trust them to handle the task.

e) Give them the authority needed to get the task done (especially in an office environment).

f) Actually give them the space to do it. Don't take the project back from them the first time they do it incorrectly or slowly. At one point, you had to learn how to do the task too, so give them time to learn and improve. Use lots of positive feedback when things are going as planned.

g) Hold them responsible for the results and deliverables. If you delegate, you MUST be willing to give feedback and hold them to deadlines. Feedback is only helpful if it is actually given.

h) Always give credit where credit is due.

ONCE YOU HAVE HANDED OVER THE RESPONSIBILITY FOR ACHIEVING THE DESIRED RESULT, FOCUS ON RESULTS AND NOT THE METHOD!

Although the method your delegate chooses to use to accomplish the task may not be the way you would have chosen, choose your battles and don't lose sight of the big picture. Their way may have worked out just fine and then you would have spent time "helping" them, when you were not needed at all for the task to be suitably completed. You can ASK them if they need resources, guidance or coaching throughout the project, but don't, whatever you do, take it back.

HOW CAN I ENSURE THEY ARE ON TRACK?

When you delegate, you should have communicated (in writing preferably) who is responsible, what is being done, when it's being done by, and how you want them to give you updates. The specifications for the updates should definitely include not just how frequently you want updates, but also what minimal information should be in the update.

Request updates on a regular basis, especially for new hires – people with whom you don't have much working experience. I would recommend a weekly update for a 6-month long project. For something that is due in 5 days. I would expect updates daily until the person had effectively handled a few projects. Hold them to the deadlines that they set for themselves, and ask for specific tasks that have been accomplished since the last update. (Do not just ask, "How's the project going?" because you'll get "fine.")

If a deadline or update is missed, you MUST address it with feedback immediately. You want success for your team members and that means holding them accountable for the responsibilities.

There you are. It is all laid out. Get yourself organized and then start handing out those tasks to whomever you can, so you can focus on the BIG goals.

As an outsider, looking at most managerial situations, it is clear that most managers and business owners do not delegate enough, even though there probably isn't a business book out there that doesn't include a chapter on using delegation as a means to get more done and develop your team. As a simple example, if you work for someone else, you can probably name at least one thing that takes up their time that you could handle for them. Similarly, don't you think that the people who work for you look up at you and probably see the tasks that are currently on your plate that they could do?

NOW IT'S YOUR TURN!

Take the first steps to letting go of at least 2 things on your plate.

Picture your daily task list and think of what you would do with a few extra hours of time!

Pick 2 small tasks from your task list that you believe you can delegate and WRITE THEM DOWN.

Task 1.)_____

Task 2.)_____

Now, who are you going to get to do these tasks?

Person for Task #1_____

Person for Task #2_____

Now, here comes the hardest part: write down when YOU will have delegated these two tasks by. Commit to taking the first step to letting go so your business can grow beyond YOU. Follow the steps above to get these items off your list!

Date I will have delegated task #1 _____

Date I will have delegated task #2 _____

Believe me, you'll feel lighter just getting a few things off your list.

Here are some resources I found REALLY helpful –

Books:

The 4-hour Work Week ~ Timothy Ferriss

80/20 Principle ~ Richard Koch

Eat That Frog!: 21 Great Ways to Stop Procrastinating and Get More Done in Less Time ~ Brian Tracy

Podcast:

Manager Tools (available on iTunes or at: www.manager-tools.com)

About Katie

Katie Hughes is an inventor and entrepreneur, whose creative ideas have built a business with a patent-pending product that protects the knees and joints of over 10,000 dance fitness instructors, and their students.

While pursuing her PhD in Chemistry from Princeton University, Katie, a certified group fitness instructor with many years of experience teaching multiple class formats, began to teach at a dance fitness class at Princeton. After several of her students complained about knee pain and expressed their reluctance to buy expensive dance shoes, the idea to create a straight-forward product that solved this problem intrigued Katie. In 2010, after receiving her PhD and while working fulltime, Katie created Slip-On Dancers™, a product that people in fitness and dance classes could wear over a regular gym shoe to safely spin and pivot on surfaces such as carpet, hardwood and rubber.

Since its introduction to the market, Katie has driven the company to spectacular growth due to creative innovation and targeted marketing. She effectively uses her scientific background and management experience to analyze the business and to focus on creating new products and line extensions for Slip-On Dancers™. She was a winner of the Make Mine a Million $ Business Competition and has been featured in Women's Entrepreneur Magazine, the Charlotte Business Journal, and USA Today. She has been an invited speaker on entrepreneurship at Princeton University.

Katie lives in Charlotte, NC with her husband and two dogs.

To learn more about Katie Hughes, Slip-On Dancers™ and how you can own a pair, visit: www.slipondancers.com or call 1-877-988-7420.